Wonders

Genre Read-Aloud

Anthology

McGraw Hill Education

mhreadingwonders.com

Send all inquiries to:
McGraw-Hill Education
2 Penn Plaza
New York, NY 10121

ISBN: 978-0-07-898220-0
MHID: 0-07-898220-0

Printed in the United States of America.

2 3 4 5 6 7 QVS 22 21 20 19 18

A

CONTENTS

Read-Alouds: An Important Component of Balanced Literacy *by Kathy Rhea Bumgardner, MEd* vi

How to Use the Genre Read–Aloud Anthology x

Poetry

Informational Text

READ-ALOUDS: AN IMPORTANT COMPONENT OF BALANCED LITERACY

by Kathy Rhea Bumgardner, MEd
National Literacy Consultant
North Carolina Educator Strategies Unlimited, Inc. Belmont, North Carolina
Creator of Think Aloud Clouds and Literacy Toolkits for Comprehension
Professional Development Videos for Instructional Best Practices in Literacy

Introduction

The read-aloud is a strategic instructional practice in which the teacher sets aside time to read texts orally to students on a consistent basis from selected various texts. The lessons are interactive and deepen students' understanding of the text through text-dependent questions.

How important is it that teachers read aloud to their students on a daily basis? How can we ensure that, with so much to accomplish in today's 21st century classrooms, the benefits of reading aloud are worth the instructional time spent in class?

Books play an important role in students' academic and social development.

Reading high-quality books increases students' overall language competence, and the process of reading, listening, questioning, and responding to a story provides a foundation for reflective and critical thinking (Pressley, 2006). Children imitate their teachers, and they are eager to read the books their teachers read (Cunningham, 2005).

The Value of the Read-Aloud

The read-aloud in today's classrooms should be a valuable and intentional part of good instruction. It can be a highly effective strategy for nurturing and developing literacy learners. It can be that match to light that love of reading fire for students.

In 1985 the report of the Commission on Reading, *Becoming a Nation of Readers,* made a lasting statement about reading aloud (p. 23). They stated: "The single most important activity for building the knowledge required for eventual success in reading is read aloud to children" (1985).

Read-alouds allow children to access more complex text than they can access while reading on their own, as well as access more complex concepts.

In the absence of the read-alouds, we may slow students' vocabulary learning; research has shown a strong positive correlation between read-aloud experiences and vocabulary development (Meehan, 1999; Roberts, 2008; Sénéchal & LeFevre, 2002; Sharif, Ozuah, Dinkevich, & Mulvihill, 2003). A well-planned read-aloud can repeatedly expose children to academic vocabulary that will likely show up in content textbooks.

Teachers can use read-alouds to increase their students' comprehension skills, foster their critical thinking through discussion and demonstration, and develop their students' background knowledge and interest in quality literature. While reading, teachers can model oral reading fluency and encourage strategies that students can implement during independent reading.

Preparing for Successful Read-Alouds

Choosing short, high quality and high interest texts is the important first step for an interactive read-aloud lesson. These texts should be complex due to structure, the use of language conventions, background knowledge, and/or levels of meaning. Providing interaction with a variety of texts is key.

High interest informational texts should be included. When Nell Duke (2000) examined the use of informational texts in 20 first-grade classrooms, she found that on average, children spent 3.6 minutes a day on informational texts, with urban schools spending 1.9 minutes a day. With the recent emphasis on a shift towards increasing informational texts, it is important to consider that balance of the genres is crucial. Encounters with high interest informational texts, as well as high quality narrative read-alouds, give depth to the read-aloud.

ILeysen/Shutterstock.com

In order to deliver an effective read-aloud, teachers should maintain a productive quality to the pacing, tone, and setting of read-aloud time to establish healthy expectations while optimizing learning potential. Teachers should consider structuring the read-aloud around skill building as much as for enjoyment (Layne, 2015).

Setting the stage for a read-aloud by including and modeling think-alouds can provide crucial scaffolding for students. The think-aloud strategy helps teachers to intentionally demonstrate for readers how to think about how they make meaning (Beers, 2003).

Strategic think alouds during the read-aloud are a way of making public the thinking that goes on inside your head as you read.

Reading aloud is still an essential tool to not only motivate readers to enjoy reading but also to assist in helping students on their academic journey to be college and career ready.

A Great Resource for Genre Focus

One of the most valuable things a teacher can do to support early readers with understanding various genres is to use read-alouds. Teachers will find that strategic read-alouds are a valuable resource for helping students to navigate their work in multiple genres.

For example, if students are reading fiction, the richness of a read-aloud can help them with key reading skills and strategies such as asking and answering questions, with a focus on characters, settings, and the major events of a story. The read-aloud time can also provide students with opportunities to have accountable collaborative conversations with their peers and teachers about the elements and deepen their comprehension.

In informational texts, the focus should be on facts and key details about the topic. This includes the importance of vocabulary and the author's sequencing of information. Through read-alouds, the students will be interactively engaged and guided to listen for those important key details.

Listening and reading for key details in fiction and informational texts are two different actions. Read-alouds can provide the teacher a consistent and strategic opportunity to allow students to both hear and discuss those key details while learning how to listen differently for, and gaining comprehension with, each genre.

The read-aloud and follow-up conversation allows teachers the opportunity to help students develop background knowledge and connect concepts so that all children can begin to clarify their thinking during their discussions with their peers and teacher (Dorn & Soffos, 2005).

Next steps:

- Pre-read and reread the selection to determine what part of the text you will read.

- Consider your reading goals and focus.

- Identify the process and strategy information (at work in the text).

- Anticipate where background knowledge needs to be built.

- Highlight places to stop for the think alouds where you can question or make meaningful connections.

- Plan for possible discussion questions before the lesson.

- Practice reading the selection using gestures and voice intonation.

- Plan for possible discussion questions before the lesson.

References

Cunningham, P. (2005). Struggling readers: "If they don't read much, how they ever gonna get good?" The Reading Teacher 59 (1): 88–90.

Pressley, M. (2006). Reading instruction that works: The case for balanced teaching, 3rd ed. New York: Guilford.

Trelease, J., & Trelease, J. (2013) The Read-Aloud Handbook- 7th Ed. New York, NY: Penquin Books.

Richard C. Anderson, Elfrieda H. Hiebert, Judith A. Scott, and Ian A. G. Wilkinson, Becoming a Nation of Readers: The Report of the Commission on Reading, U. S. Department of Education (Champaign-Urbana, IL: Center for the Study of Reading, 1985), p. 23.

Layne, S. (2015) In defense of read aloud-sustaining best practice. Stenhouse Publishers (town?)

Beers, K. (2003). When kids can't read, what teachers can do. Portsmouth, NH: Heinemann, p. 101.

Duke, N. K. (2000). 3.6 minutes per day: The scarcity of informational texts in first grade. Reading Research Quarterly, 35(2), 202–224.

Meehan, M. L. (1999). Evaluation of the Monomgalia County schools' Even Start program child vocabulary outcomes. Charleston, WV: AEL.

Roberts, T. (2008). Home storybook reading in primary or second language preschool children: Evidence of equal effectiveness for second language vocabulary acquisition. Reading Research Quarterly, 43(2), 103–130.

Sénéchal, M., & LeFevre, J. A. (2002). Parental involvement in the development of children's reading skill: A five year longitudinal study. Child Development, 73(2), 445–460.

Sharif, I., Ozuah, P. O., Dinkevich, E. I., & Mulvihill, M. (2003). Impact of a brief literacy intervention on urban preschoolers. Early Childhood Education Journal, 30(3), 177–180.

Dorn, L., & Soffos, C. (2005). Teaching for deep comprehension. Portland, ME: Stenhouse.

HOW TO USE THE GENRE READ–ALOUD ANTHOLOGY

Key Features of the Genre Read–Aloud Anthology

- The selections in this anthology feature engaging read–aloud experiences in a variety of genres.

- The selections in the book are grouped together by genres.

- Each selection includes 2–4 color images that can be shown while reading.

- The selections include instructional prompts at point-of-use:
  - Genre feature box that focuses on an aspect of the genre
  - Think-alouds demonstrating how to use comprehension skills and strategies with the stories
  - Questions that focus on genre features
  - Questions about the text
  - Oral vocabulary words that have been highlighted in the text with child-friendly definitions

Tips for Using the Genre Read–Aloud Anthology

Choose a Story

This anthology has been designed for flexible use. The stories are organized by genre, so pick one to enhance your genre focus. You can also find stories that support themes, incorporate skills and strategies, and other instructional goals.

Preview the Story

Reading the story ahead of time will help you to anticipate background knowledge gaps. It will also help you decide where to pause for emphasis and where to elicit questions, predictions, or reactions. You may even want to practice reading it aloud.

Preview the Instructional Prompts

Preview the sidebar prompts to think about when you want to use them.

Read with Expression

Let your voice reflect the tone of the story or the personalities of the characters. Don't read too fast. Vary your pace so you can pause for emphasis. Allow time for children to think about what's happening or what might come next.

Model Your Own Engagement

Model your own reading process, focusing on language patterns or phrases you liked or parts of the text that made you feel or visualize something. Talk about what you notice. Model using the vocabulary words.

Encourage Children to Participate

Allow time for children to look at the pictures, make comments, and ask questions. Invite them to make predictions and share ideas about how the characters changed, or to talk about new information presented. Encourage them to use the vocabulary words.

Reread

Rereading the selection is recommended. Rereading is a good opportunity to focus on instruction, to ask questions about comprehension, and to clarify aspects of the text that may be confusing. You may also choose passages to reread that require more attention.

Genre

Realistic Fiction:
Realistic fiction is a made-up story with characters, settings, and events that could happen in real life.

Realistic Fiction

What details could happen in real life?

wide: open as much as possible

Key Details

Think Aloud

Key details in the words and pictures help us understand the story. The text says that Lily is worried that her teacher will forget her name. This is a key detail because it tells me that Lily is nervous about what will happen on her first day. Let's look for other key details as we read.

Lily's First Day

Today is the first day of school. Lily lies in bed for a while. Her eyes are **wide** open. She wonders what first grade will be like.

"Lily, come down to breakfast!" calls Mom. "You don't want to be late on the first day."

Lily slips on her shirt that says LILY in big purple letters and goes downstairs.

"Why don't you wear your new outfit?" asks Mom.

"What if my teacher can't remember my name?" Lily asks.

Lily's mom offers her a pancake and gives her a kiss.

"Don't worry," she says. "First grade will be just fine."

But Lily keeps her LILY shirt on.

Just in case.

"It's time to leave," says Dad.

Lily runs to her room. She stuffs Purple, her elephant, in her pocket.

"I think Purple may be too little to go to school," says Dad.

"But what if no one in first grade wants to play with me?" Lily asks.

Lily's Dad gives her a big hug. "Don't worry so much," he says. "First grade will be just fine."

But Lily **tucks** Purple's trunk inside her pocket.

Just in case.

On the way to school, Lily sings the ABC song.

"I haven't heard you sing that in a long time," says Dad.

"I know," says Lily. "But what if we have to know it for first grade?"

Dad smiles. "Don't be **nervous** Lily," he says. "First grade will be just fine."

But Lily finishes the ABC song quietly to herself.

Just in case.

Visualize

Think Aloud

When we visualize, we create pictures in our minds of what is happening in the story. In our minds, we can see the characters and what they're doing. Here the author says that Dad hugs Lily. When I close my eyes, I can see the hug and it helps me understand that Dad is trying to soothe Lily, who is very nervous. Let's keep visualizing as we read on.

tucks: pushes in so that you can't see it

nervous: having uncomfortable feelings

arrive: get to a place

Key Details

What happens when Lily looks around the room? Why is this a key detail?

At last, they **arrive** at first grade.

"Hello, Lily," says her new teacher. "Welcome to first grade! I like your shirt."

Lily likes her teacher's smile. She likes her cat pin and her striped socks.

She looks around the room. She likes all the books, some thick with chapters. She likes the games and puzzles and the markers in her favorite colors. She likes the long lined paper for writing real stories.

"You can hang your backpack in the closet by your name," says her teacher.

Lily walks toward the closet. She sticks her hand in her pocket so she can hold Purple for a few seconds. She passes an art area that has colorful papers and new markers set up. Lily wonders if she will get to draw today.

Lily hangs up her backpack in the closet. She notices that next to her name is the name "Lulu."

"Who is Lulu?" she wonders. She tells herself that first grade will be just fine and squeezes Purple one more time.

Just in case.

Her teacher rings a bell. "Welcome class," she says. "Let's meet on the rug and we can all get to know each other."

Lily finds a good spot. She takes Purple out to keep her company.

"I have an elephant just like yours."

Lily looks up and sees a girl with LULU written in big red letters on her shirt. Lulu smiles. She has a big **gap** where a tooth used to be.

"Oops," says Lulu covering her mouth. "What if none of the other kids lost a tooth?"

Lily picks up Purple to make room for Lulu.

"Don't worry," says Lily. "First grade will be just fine."

And somehow she knows it will be.

gap: empty space

Visualize

Can you picture Lulu covering her mouth as she says "oops"? Why do you think she does that? What is she feeling?

Genre

Realistic Fiction: This genre is a made-up story with characters, setting, and events that could happen in real life. Realistic fiction has a problem and solution. It can have characters that use their imaginations.

Character, Setting, and Events

Think Aloud

As we read, we think about the people, places, and events in the story. I learned that Mrs. Garcia is in the classroom with her students, and Finn is one of her students. Let's keep thinking about these characters, what they do, and where they are in the story as we continue reading.

prepare: to get ready

Finn's Perfect Job

"Boys and girls," says Mrs. Garcia, "this week, we're going to talk about jobs in the community. To **prepare**, I would like to know what job you would like to do when you grow up."

Everyone's hands shoot up in the air. All but Finn's.

"I want to be a bus driver," says Avery. "They get to drive all over town."

Ezra goes next. "I want to be a mail carrier."

Sophia waves her hand. "I want to be a dentist, just like my mom."

"I want to be a chef and cook delicious food," says Jasper.

"Finn," says Mrs. Garcia, "What do you want to be?"

Finn frowns and shrugs. He had never thought about it before. "I don't know."

Mrs. Garcia asks him to keep thinking about it. He'll figure out something.

At recess, the kids pretend they're doing their future jobs.

"Watch your step!" says Avery, as she pretends to open the bus door.

Finn pretends to drive a bus, too. "Vroom-vroom!" He almost runs into Jack! Then he remembers when he crashed his race car into the garage door and the wheels fell off.

Hmm, he thinks, *that's not the job for me.*

"Here's your mail!" says Ezra.

Finn helps **deliver** the mail. "Ding-dong! Mailman!" he calls. But then Jack pretends he's a barking dog. Finn thinks about his dog Buster chasing Mr. Paul, his mailman, all the way down the street, nipping at his heels.

Hmm, he thinks, *that's not the job for me either.*

deliver: to take something to someone

Make and Confirm Predictions

Think Aloud

When we read, we can guess what will happen next by thinking about the text and the illustrations. Then we can read on to see if our prediction is correct. I think that Finn will think about being a dentist next because he has already tried out being a bus driver and mailman. What is your prediction? Let's continue reading to find out if our predictions are correct.

Make and Confirm Predictions

I predicted that Finn would pretend to be a dentist next. I read that Sophia asks Finn if he wants to be a dentist and she says "Open wide!" My prediction was correct. Was your prediction correct? Let's make another prediction. What might happen next in the story?

Realistic Fiction

How are the characters using their imagination?

disappointed: feeling unhappy because something you hoped for did not happen

slumps: moves shoulders down suddenly

Sophia asks Finn if he wants to be a dentist. "Open wide!" she says.

Finn imagines putting his fingers inside someone else's mouth. Ooey, gooey, slimy. ICK!

That's definitely not the job for me, he thinks, feeling **disappointed**.

Finn kicks a small rock. *There has to be something I can do.*

Jasper pretends he's cooking on a hot grill. Finn pretends to cook but remembers the time he tried to make a special breakfast for Mom on her birthday. Good thing Dad knew how to get jam and butter off the ceiling.

Hmm, he thinks, *I'm not good at anything.*

The bell rings. Finn **slumps** and is last in line to go back into the classroom.

During free time, Finn sits alone at the art table. He picks up his favorite purple crayon and starts to draw pictures of all his friends doing their jobs. Avery the bus driver. Ezra the mail carrier. Sophia the dentist. Jasper the chef.

Finn frowns. *But what can I do?*

Avery walks over and looks at Finn's work. "That's really good! I'm driving a bus!"

Soon, Ezra, Sophia, and Jasper crowd around Finn. "Awesome! Cool!"

"You're really good at drawing," says Jasper.

"Really?" Finn says. He loves to draw. He imagines what it would be like to do that all the time. *That* would be fun!

He looks at the class bookshelf full of beautiful books. His hand shoots up in the air.

"Yes, Finn," says Mrs. Garcia.

"I know what I want to be!" says Finn. "I want to be an **illustrator**!"

Yes, he thinks, *the perfect job for me!*

Character, Setting, and Events
How does the setting change in the story? Why is the change important?

Character, Setting, and Events
What event helps Finn decide what he wants to be when he grows up?

illustrator: the person who draws the pictures in a book

Make and Confirm Predictions
Have partners confirm the predictions they made.

Genre

Realistic Fiction: This genre is a made up story with characters, settings, and events that could happen in real life.

invited: asked to come

chefs: people who cook in a restaurant

Character, Setting, and Events

Think Aloud

Remember that learning about the setting can help us understand the story. When I look at the picture, I learn that Mateo lives on a farm. There are trees, a barn, and a windmill near his house. Let's look for more information about the setting, as well as characters and events, as we continue reading.

County Fair, City Fair

One afternoon, Mateo gets a letter from his cousin Isabella, who lives in the city. Mateo starts to read.

Dear Mateo,

It's almost time for our City Fair, and you are invited! It's my favorite time of the year. There are no cars allowed, and everyone walks in the streets. All the chefs let you try their special dishes. We get to eat food from around the world! Musicians come to play the best music, such as jazz, rock and roll, and more. There are also rides and games. The whole city will be there, and everyone wears City Fair T-shirts. The fair is on August 21. I really hope you can come. Write back soon!

Isabella

Mateo quickly writes back.

Dear Isabella,

The City Fair sounds amazing! One day I'd love to go with you. But August 21 is when we have our County Fair. It's my favorite event of the whole year, and you are invited! Our fair sounds different from yours. We have a big celebration with all the farmers and their farm animals. Instead of city streets, we have huge tents and barns and fenced in areas for the animals. I'm bringing my pig, Priscilla! The county bakers have a big apple pie contest. Yum! Then there's a rodeo with lots of cowboys. We have a barbeque and country music. And the night ends with a big dance. The whole county will be there, and everyone wears a special hat. We would love it if you came. Priscilla would love it, too! Write back soon!

Mateo

PS: Priscilla says "snort," which means "hi!"

Realistic Fiction

How do you know that events in this story could happen in real life?

celebration: party for a special occasion

Make and Confirm Predictions

Think Aloud

Remember that we can make predictions about what will happen next. I predict that when Isabella writes back to Mateo, she will tell him that she can't come. I'll read on to see if my prediction is correct. What do you predict will happen next?

Make and Confirm Predictions

My prediction was correct. When Isabella wrote back, she said that she couldn't go to County Fair. Was your prediction correct? What do you think will happen next?

Character, Setting, and Events

What is one thing you learn about Isabella from her letter?

slice: a piece of food cut from something

Dear Mateo,

Your County Fair sounds like so much fun. And it does sound totally different from City Fair. I wish I could see it for myself, but I can't come because my fair is on the same weekend. It would have been great to meet your pig, Priscilla, and help you feed her in the barn. I also want a BIG slice of one of those apple pies. I have never seen a real rodeo. Wow! I would love one of those special hats, too. It could say "Isabella" in pink, my favorite color! I can't believe City Fair and County Fair are both on August 21. I will send you the City Fair T-shirt.

Isabella

Dear Isabella,

Wait a minute! Our County Fair is August 1, not August 21! That's three whole weeks apart! So Dad says we can come with you to City Fair after all. And I'm sure your mom will allow you to come to our fair. Now we can be together for BOTH of our favorite events of the year. This is going to be the best August ever!

Mateo

Which is exactly what it was. And so was every August after that, when Isabella and Mateo enjoyed each other's fairs.

Character, Setting, and Events
What important event happens in this part of the story?

allow: to let someone do something

Make and Confirm Predictions
Have partners confirm their predictions.

Genre

Realistic Fiction: This genre has made-up stories that have characters, settings, and events that can exist in real life.

gentle: soft, not rough

blushes: turns red in the face

Plot: Problem and Solution

Think Aloud

A problem is something characters want to do, change, or find out. The way the problem is solved is the solution. I see Chen's problem. He taps out the sounds he hears when he should be doing other things. As I continue to read, let's listen for how Chen solves his problem.

Chen the Tapper

"*Tick-Tock, Tick-Tock!*" Chen listens to the clock at the front of the classroom.

He picks up his pencil and starts to tap on his desk.

"*Tick-Tock, Tick-Tock,*" says the clock. "*Tip-Tap, Tip-Tap,*" says Chen's pencil.

He closes his eyes. A clock song! Chen smiles.

Then he feels a **gentle** hand on his shoulder.

"Chen," says Miss Carter. "Please stop tapping. It's time for math."

Chen **blushes** and puts down his pencil. "I'm sorry, Miss Carter."

Soon the buzzer sounds. It's time for recess. "Everyone line up quietly," says Miss Carter.

Chen picks up a ruler as he gets in line. He taps it on the wall. *Buzz! Buzz! Buzz!* He closes his eyes and repeats it. A buzzer song!

At recess, Chen and his friends play on the swings. Chen pumps his legs as hard as he can. **Suddenly**, he hears a bird call: *Caw Caw Caw Caw.* He hops off the swing and starts tapping his foot. *Caw Caw Caw Caw.* He begins to tap harder. *CAW CAW CAW.* He smiles. A bird song!

All of a sudden, Chen realizes what he is doing. He looks around, **embarrassed**. He joins his friends for a game of soccer. Now there is no way he can tap out sounds!

When recess is over, Chen walks slowly across the playground. He notices something different. The big kids are all singing and dancing. They look as if they are having so much fun. For the first time, he wishes he could be a big kid. He starts to tap his foot. He thinks and taps.

"Chen," say the other kids. "Stop tapping so we can go inside."

"I'm sorry," says Chen. "I won't tap anymore." Chen sighs. No matter how hard he tries, he can't help listening to the sounds all around him and then tapping them out.

Plot: Problem and Solution

Think Aloud

Chen tries to solve his problem by playing with his friends. He thinks this will stop him from tapping.

Realistic Fiction
How do you know this story is realistic fiction?

We can ask questions as we read and then look for the answers. I wonder what Chen will do with the paper plates and dried beans. I will continue reading to see if my question is answered. As I read, think of your own questions and listen for the answers.

practices: does something again and again to get better at it

scrambled: moved quickly

After school, Chen has an idea. It may be the best idea he has ever had!

"May I have some paper plates and dried beans?" he asks his dad.

"What for?" asks Dad. Chen whispers his secret to him.

"Interesting," says Dad.

Chen puts beans between two plates. He tapes the edges of the plates to seal it. He shakes it. "Yes!"

"May I borrow the mop bucket and wooden spoons?" he asks his mom.

"What for?" asks Mom. Chen whispers his secret to her.

"Good thinking!" says Mom.

All afternoon Chen **practices**. The next day Chen's dad helps him carry his things to school in a big sack. Chen gets through math without tapping. He lines up for recess without tapping.

Even Miss Carter notices. "Chen, I like the way you **scrambled** to get into line just now. Good work!" Chen smiles.

Once outside, all of Miss Carter's class plays tag. All but Chen. He pulls the bucket and wooden spoons out of his bag. He gives it a tap. He pulls out the paper plates and beans. He gives it a shake. Then he starts to play.

Tip-Tap, Tip-Tap! He thinks about the clock. *Buzz! Buzz! Buzz!* He thinks about the buzzer. *Caw Caw Caw!* He thinks about the bird song. He closes his eyes and thinks of all of his favorite sounds. He taps louder. He taps faster. Soon the big kids are dancing. Then the first graders stop playing tag. They listen and they start to dance. Even the teachers **stomp** to the beat.

"Who is that little kid with the great beats?" ask the big kids.

"That is Chen the Tapper!" says Chen's classmates.

Chen hears this. "Uh-oh," he thinks. He stops tapping.

"Chen!" call the kids. "Don't stop tapping! You're playing great music! We want to dance!"

And that is just what Chen does.

Ask and Answer Questions

Think Aloud

I noticed the answer to my question. Chen shakes the plates with the beans inside. He's making music. Remember to listen for answers to your questions.

Plot: Problem and Solution
Now that you know Chen's problem and the steps he took to solve it, what is his solution?

stomp: to put your foot down forcefully

Genre

Realistic Fiction: This genre is a made-up story with characters, settings, and events that could happen in real life.

Realistic Fiction

How do you know this story is realistic fiction?

beams: smiles happily

Springtime for Daisy

"Spring starts tomorrow," says Daisy's mom. Daisy bounces up and down on her bed.

"I can't wait," says Daisy. "In spring, I can go out and pick my favorite flower. Can you guess which one?"

"Hmm," says Daisy's mom. "Is it a daisy?"

"Yes!" Daisy **beams**. "It matches my name! I'm going outside to find spring daisies first thing tomorrow."

"You'll have to see what the weather is like," says Daisy's mom. "It might not be a good day for flower-picking. But there are other fun things you can do. Now get some sleep." Daisy's mom kisses her goodnight.

And Daisy thinks of finding daisies.

The next morning, a light frost covers the ground in Daisy's part of the **country**. A few snowflakes drift down from the sky, swirling in the chilly air. They gather on the ground forming a thin layer of white.

"I guess it's not a good day for flower-picking," Daisy moans.

"I'm afraid not," says Daisy's mom. "But it *is* a great day for making shapes in the snow!"

Daisy puts on her puffy coat and mittens and goes outside. She sees her breath **form** clouds in the cold air. She lies down in the snow and moves her arms and legs. She catches snowflakes on her tongue.

At bedtime, her mom asks, "How was your day?"

"It was fun to play in the snow, but I didn't find any daisies. That's all I really want."

"Maybe next week," her mom says, and kisses her goodnight.

Daisy dreams of finding daisies.

country: land where a group of people live

form: make

Plot: Cause and Effect

Think Aloud

Remember that a cause is the reason why something happens. The effect is what happens. I read that it's snowing in Daisy's part of the country. That is the cause. Daisy makes shapes in the snow. That's the effect. Listen for other causes and effects as I read.

grumpy: in a bad mood

Visualize

Think Aloud

Remember that the author uses words that help us picture in our minds what is happening. When I close my eyes, I can see water dripping from the leaves on the trees drip, drip, drip. As I continue reading, picture the setting and the events in your mind.

The next week, rain pours down. The leaves on the trees drip, drip, drip, and the ground is wet and muddy.

"I guess it's not a good day for flower-picking," Daisy moans, feeling **grumpy**.

"I'm afraid not," says Daisy's mom. "But it *is* a great day for puddle-jumping!"

Daisy puts on her raincoat and rain boots and goes outside. She dances between the raindrops. She splashes in the puddles. She squishes in the mud.

At bedtime, her mom asks, "How was your day?"

"It was fun to play in the rain, but I didn't find any daisies. That's all I really want."

"Give it time," her mom says, and kisses her goodnight.

And Daisy dreams of finding daisies.

Many weeks pass as Daisy waits, dreaming each night of picking her favorite flower. One day the wind is blowing. The trees sway back and forth, and the wind blows the clouds across the sky.

"Would you like to fly your kite? It's a great day for kite-flying!" Mom exclaims.

Daisy puts on her jacket, grabs her kite, and she and mom go outside. Daisy flies her kite high in the sky. She and mom run with it and watch it race along beside them. But then a strong **gust** blows the kite right out of Daisy's hand! She and mom run after it, but it seems to blow farther and farther away.

Finally, Daisy finds her kite. It is resting on a **patch** of little daisies just starting to bloom!

"Mom, look what I found!" cries Daisy. She **gathers** a few and shows them to her mom.

"Well, look at that," her mom says. At home that night, Daisy looks at her beautiful daisies until she falls fast asleep.

Plot: Cause and Effect
What happened on page 20 that caused Mom to suggest kite flying?

Visualize
Can you picture Daisy looking at her beautiful daisies until she falls asleep? What do you think she's feeling?

gust: a sudden rush of strong wind

patch: a small spot different from the rest of an area

gathers: brings into one place

Genre

Realistic Fiction:
Realistic fiction is a
made-up story with
characters, settings,
and events that could
happen in real life.
Realistic fiction can
also have characters
that use their
imaginations.

Realistic Fiction

*What makes this story
realistic fiction?*

chilly: cool

A Tasty Family Tradition

One winter afternoon, Miles and his Grandpa Mac are sitting on the couch reading a story. All of a sudden a gusty wind comes whipping through the house.

"Brrr," says Miles. "It's kind of cold."

"I'd say it's downright **chilly**," says Grandpa Mac. "Do you know what our family has always done when it's chilly?"

"What?" asks Miles.

"Make chili!" says Grandpa Mac. "It's a family tradition. I think we have everything we need. Let's go to the kitchen and make some!"

Grandpa Mac goes to the refrigerator and takes out a few ingredients. Then he takes out a pot and starts to cook.

"When I was a little boy," says Grandpa Mac. "My grandpa taught me how to make our family's **traditional** chili. It was very **simple**. He used only a few ingredients such as meat, beans, tomatoes, onions, salt, and pepper."

"That *is* easy!" says Miles.

"And tasty," says Grandpa Mac. "We thought that **nobody** could make chili as well as my grandpa. But my dad thought he could make it just a bit better. So he added chili peppers."

"Mmm," says Miles. "That does sound good."

"It *was!*" says Grandpa Mac. "So adding chili peppers became a new family tradition."

"Coooooooooooool," says Miles.

traditional: doing something that has been done in a family for a long time

simple: easy to do

nobody: no one

Theme

Think Aloud

Remember that the theme is the message the author wants to share. As I read, I look for clues to help me identify the theme. I read that Grandpa Mac's grandpa taught him how to make the family's chili recipe. That is a clue that will help me understand the theme. As I read, listen for more clues.

suggested: gave an idea for others to think about

Theme

What happens to the chili as it is passed down from one person to another in the family?

Visualize

Think Aloud

As I read about Miles' dad adding chocolate to the chili recipe, I can picture a young boy dropping spoonfuls of cocoa into the pot and stirring. This helps me understand how Miles' dad changed the family recipe. Let's continue to visualize as we read the story.

"*Chili* cool!" says Grandpa. "But I thought maybe I could make it just a bit better. So I added a little brown sugar and some sausage."

"Mmm," says Miles, as Grandpa Mac adds the brown sugar and sausage. "That sounds yummy!"

"It *was* yummy," says Grandpa Mac, as he stirs in the new ingredients. "So it became part of the family tradition. Your father loved that chili, too. But he thought he might make it just a bit better. You'll never guess what he **suggested**."

"Tell me!" shouts Miles.

"Your father added cocoa," says Grandpa Mac.

"You mean, like chocolate?" asks Miles, giggling.

"That's exactly what I mean," says Grandpa Mac. "And you know what? It was delicious! And now it's a tradition."

The kitchen starts to smell wonderful. "The chili is almost ready," says Grandpa Mac. "Would you like to add something all your own?"

Miles thinks about it. It is **difficult** to know what to add! The chili already has so many good things in it. What could Miles **possibly** add? For a moment, he imagines adding his favorite food—apples!

Then he has an idea. Miles runs to the refrigerator and gets grated cheese and sour cream, and grabs a bag of tortilla chips. "I think these should go on top," he says.

"Well that *is* a great idea," says Grandpa Mac. He scoops the chili into two big bowls, and Miles adds his toppings.

"YUM!" they both say at the same time.

"You know what?" asks Grandpa. "You made our family chili even better!"

"I did?" asks Miles with a big smile.

"You did," says Grandpa. "And this will be our new family tradition—the perfect chili to make on a chilly day."

Visualize

Miles imagines adding apples to the chili. What do you picture in your mind about this?

difficult: hard

possibly: used to say that something might be done but is not certain

Theme

Think of the clues the author has given us about Miles, Grandpa Mac, and the family chili recipe. What is the theme of the story?

Genre

Fantasy: A fantasy is a story that has made-up characters, settings, or other elements that could not exist in real life.

Fantasy

What details could not exist in real life?

Visualize

Think Aloud

Remember that when we visualize, we think about the author's words and then create a picture in our minds of what is happening in the story. The author describes Oliver's new apartment building. In my mind, I can see how tall it is and how different it is from Oliver's home in the small town.

residents: people living in a certain place

Oliver in the City

Oliver is a happy small-town rabbit. He has always lived in a small town. And he has always liked living there. But today, Oliver and Mom are moving to the BIG city.

The birds sing a goodbye song. "TWEET! TWEET! Goodbye, Oliver!"

"Will the big city be the same as a small town?" Oliver asks.

"Some things will be the same," says Mom, "and some will be different."

Their new apartment building is so tall Oliver can't even see the roof. There is no front porch for Oliver to race his trucks. Instead, there is an elevator to take the residents up and down.

"It's not the same as our house," Oliver says.

The next morning, Oliver looks outside. He sees many yellow taxis and long buses in the street. He hears loud horns.

HONK! HONK!

Mom and Oliver ride the city bus. The bus makes many stops, and people get on and off.

Oliver pushes the button, and a sign lights up to tell the bus driver they want to get off.

"It's not the same as our car," Oliver says. "But I like pushing the button on the bus."

"Look, here's the lake," Mom says. They get off the bus and Oliver runs to the water. But no one is swimming in the lake. Instead, some rabbits sit beside it and have a picnic. Other rabbits sail **miniature** sailboats.

"It's not the same as our lake," Oliver says.

Then someone taps his shoulder.

Oliver turns around. A rabbit his age says, "Hello. My name is Ralph. Do you like to **sail**?"

"Um . . ." Oliver says.

"It's easy," says Ralph. He shows Oliver his remote control box. "These buttons make the boat move. Do you want to try?"

"Thanks," says Oliver. He makes the sailboat **zip** across the lake.

Oliver, Ralph, and their moms take the bus home.

"I live in this apartment building," says Oliver, as they get off the bus.

"I live here, too," says Ralph. "Do you want to play?"

Oliver and Ralph go and play together.

"It's not the same as our old house," Oliver says to Ralph. "But I like this big apartment building, where I can visit a friend without going outside."

Then Oliver and Ralph hear people playing drums.

sail: make a boat move on the water

zip: move quickly

Visualize

Can you picture Oliver talking to Ralph about his new home? How do you think Oliver feels?

BOOM! BOOM!

Oliver looks out the window and sees a colorful parade of musicians **marching** down the street.

"It's not the same as our birds," Oliver says. "But I like having a parade outside my window."

"We have birds here, too," Ralph tells Oliver. "Do you want to see them?"

Oliver and Ralph take the elevator to the top floor of their building. From there, Oliver can see the big city spread out below. He sees the buses moving along the busy streets. He sees the lake with the sailboats and the musicians parading down the street.

TWEET! TWEET!

"I hear birds singing," Oliver says.

"How do you like your new home?" Ralph asks.

"Some things are the same, and some are different," Oliver says. "I'll always be a small-town rabbit, but I think I'm going to like the big city!"

marching: moving in step with others

Key Details
What sound does Oliver hear from the top floor? Why is this a key detail?

Genre

Fantasy: A story that has made-up characters, settings, or events that could not exist in real life.

Key Details

Think Aloud

Remember that the key details are the most important things that happen in a story. I noticed that Alex tells Randy that he forgets how to add numbers. It is important because Alex feels as if he hasn't learned anything since he started first grade. He is not feeling good about himself. Let's look for other key details as we read the story.

plenty: all that you need

Fantasy

Look at the illustration. How do you know that this is a fantasy?

First Grade Is Great!

Alex and his buddy Randy look at the math problem written on the rock. "I keep forgetting how to add ten plus five," moans Alex. "I feel as if I can never get it right!"

"I'm so sorry, Alex," says Randy. "I guess it takes time. I still have trouble subtracting numbers!"

"Yeah, but we've been adding numbers since kindergarten!" Alex says sadly as they walk to lunch. "I feel as if I haven't learned a thing since we started first grade."

"That's not true," says Randy. "You've learned **plenty**."

"Like what?" asks Alex.

2

"Remember the first week of school when you couldn't write the name of that character you created?" asks Randy.

Alex scoffs, "So?"

"Well, now you can write the name of the character and even a few words about it!" exclaims Randy. "And remember that time when you couldn't read more than just a few words at a time?"

"Don't remind me," Alex sighs.

"I *am* going to remind you! You were pretty **upset**, but you kept trying and trying and . . ."

"And I finally did it!" Alex interrupts.

"See?" says Randy. "You've learned more than you think."

"Maybe," says Alex, as he **nibbles** on a fly.

upset: unhappy

nibbles: eats with small, quick bites

Visualize

Think Aloud

Remember that it is important to visualize, or make pictures in our minds, when we read. I read that Alex got upset when he could read only a few words at a time, but he kept trying. When I close my eyes, I can see Alex trying so hard to read and getting upset with himself. Visualizing this scene helps me understand more about Alex. Let's keep visualizing as we read.

3

Visualize

What do you picture in your mind when I read about Alex trudging along with the "weight of the world on his shoulders"? Why does he feel this way?

results: information learned at the end of something, such as a science experiment

insists: says in a way that does not let someone disagree

Key Details

How did Alex help out with the science experiment?

After school, Alex and Randy meet their moms for the walk home. Alex trudges along as if he has the weight of the world on his shoulders.

Then their classmate Mara passes by. "Hey, Alex," she says. "Do you want to come over at 4:00 and play soccer? You can come, too, Randy."

"Yes!" they both say. Mara waves goodbye and continues on home.

"I just remember something else you learned," says Randy.

"What?" asks Alex.

"Don't you remember when we worked with Mara on that science project? You were the one who figured out all of the things that we could use for our 'Does It Float or Sink?' chart. And you drew pictures of our results!" says Randy.

"Well, I really like science," says Alex.

"Yes, and the teacher chose our project to display at the end," Randy insists. "You really helped us!

"I guess so," says Alex.

Alex and Randy continue walking until Alex looks at his watch. "Hey, we've got to hurry to get home and then get to Mara's by 4:00. It's already 3:15!"

"See," says Randy. "Could you read a watch a year ago?"

"No way," says Alex.

"Right. So now you can tell time, read, write, and do science experiments. So do you feel better now?"

"I do feel better," says Alex. "I also feel a lot smarter! Thanks, Randy. You really are a great friend! We have both had a great start to first grade after all, haven't we?"

Randy smiles. "Yes, we have!"

Key Details
What else did Alex learn to do in first grade? Why is this important?

Genre

Fantasy: A fantasy is a story with made-up characters, settings, or events that could not exist in real life.

Fantasy

What event could not happen in real life?

Character, Setting, Plot

Think Aloud

When we read, we think about the plot, or what happens in the story. I read that Sammy stayed up too late. He was so tired the next morning, he didn't wake up when his alarm went off. This is important because it leads to the next event. Sammy misses the bus. Let's keep reading to find out other events in Sammy's life.

Fifteen Minutes Late

Tick. Tock. Sammy the Squirrel stays up late reading in his bedroom. He stays up so late that he only gets four hours of sleep. The next morning he is exhausted and sleeps right through his alarm clock. "Hurry up, Sammy," yells his mother. "You're going to be late!"

Sure enough, the school bus honks as Sammy is just about to eat breakfast. His mother tosses him a sunflower seed to eat on the bus as he dashes outside. But all he sees is the school bus turning the corner in the distance. "I needed another fifteen minutes," whispers Sammy.

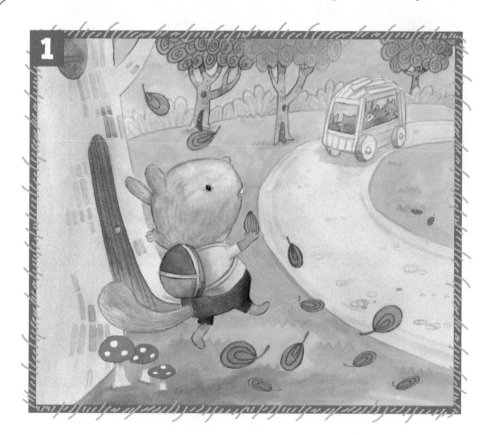

2

Sammy grabs the acorn he wanted to share at Show and Tell and hops in his mother's car. They speed off to school, but Sammy is still late. He is so late he missed Show and Tell, his favorite part of the day. "Fifteen minutes earlier," says his teacher, "and you would have made it."

At recess, Sammy climbs a tree. He begins watching a caterpillar crawl on a branch. He is so **absorbed** in the caterpillar's movements that he doesn't hear the recess bell. And Sammy is so tired he falls asleep.

Fifteen minutes later, he wakes up. He looks around. The schoolyard is silent. He hops down from the tree and runs inside the classroom.

"You have been **tardy** to class twice today, Sammy," says his teacher. "You'll need to stay after school to finish your work."

absorbed: took up all of one's attention

tardy: late

Reread

Think Aloud

Remember that we can go back and reread parts of a story we don't understand. I'm not sure why Sammy was late going back into class after recess, so I read that section again. Now I understand that he was watching a caterpillar and didn't hear the bell. Then he fell asleep. Listen as I continue reading. If you don't understand something, ask me to stop and reread some of the text.

toughest: strongest, hardest to beat

begs: asks for something in an eager way

Reread

Remember to ask me to reread any parts of the story that you don't understand.

Character, Setting, Plot

What event at the soccer field really bothers Sammy? What does Sammy realize?

Sammy frowns. Now he is going to be late for the big soccer game against the **toughest** team in town—the Purple Team. "That's probably okay," he thinks. "I'm the fastest and best player on the Green Team. They won't mind if I'm a few minutes late." But when Sammy arrives at the soccer field, the teams are already playing. And the Green Team is losing by three points!

"Let me get in the game, Coach," Sammy **begs**.

"Sorry, Sammy, but you know the rules. If you're late to the game, you sit out for the first half."

"Oh no," says Sammy. He can only sit and watch as the Purple Team scores one goal after another against his team. When Sammy finally gets to play, it is too late. His team never catches up. "If only you had been here fifteen minutes earlier," say his teammates.

When Sammy gets home, his father is busy preparing dinner. The family gathers around the table to eat yummy pecan pizza. "I think I'm going to bed," **mumbles** Sammy after eating just one slice.

"My goodness," says Sammy's mother. "What's wrong? You never eat just one slice, and it's three hours before bedtime!"

Sammy sighs. "I was late for everything today. Maybe if I get to bed early, I'll be on time tomorrow!"

"Yes," says his father. "Get a good night's rest and tomorrow everything will run like clockwork."

And it does.

Character, Setting, Plot

What important event happens at the end of the story? What does this tell you about Sammy?

mumbles: speaks low and unclearly

Ant's Picnic

Ant is crawling on a leaf when he spots a family eating a lovely meal on the grass. "A picnic!" Ant cries as he runs to the feast. He crawls off the leaf and heads toward a delicious-looking bread crumb.

He is just about to pick it up, when he hears a booming voice from above, "Ants! Ants! Ants! We're **surrounded** by ants!"

Just as Ant looks up, a large hand reaches down from the sky to swat him away. Ant quickly skitters away into the grass to hide. Now the boy and girl are both complaining about the ant, saying, "Yuck! Ants! Quick! Put the food away!"

The parents rush to put all the food away and then the whole family quickly leaves the park.

Ant feels terrible.

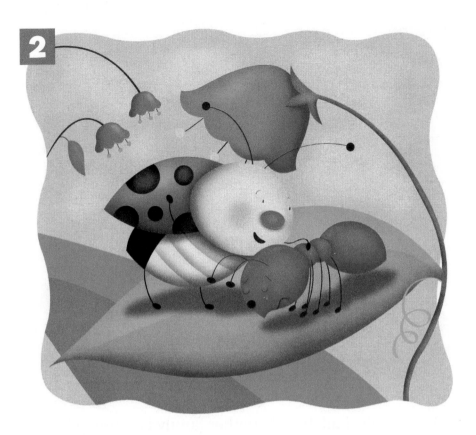

2

Ant's friend, Ladybug, flies down into the grass next to him. "What's wrong?" she asks.

"People really don't like ants."

"I'm sorry," Ladybug says.

"You're lucky, Ladybug. You are bright red and **beautiful**. Farmers want you in their gardens. Children *ooh* and *ahh* when they see you flying about. Why are you so **popular** and I'm not?"

"Well, I don't bite people. There's that," says Ladybug.

"I only bite when they want to hurt me," whispers Ant.

Ladybug continues, "I also help the farmers because I eat **pests** that nibble on their plants."

"I can't do any of that," says Ant. His head sinks lower, and he begins trudging home.

beautiful: very pretty

popular: liked by a lot of people

pests: insects or animals that can hurt plants and other living things

Point of View

Think Aloud

Point of view is the way a character thinks or feels. We learn how a character thinks or feels by what the character says and does. Ant says, "People really don't like ants." This tells me Ant's point of view about how people feel about ants. Let's think more about the characters' point of view as we continue reading.

Fantasy

Who is Ant talking to? How do we know this is a fantasy story?

3

Point of View

How is Ladybug's point of view about people different from Ant's?

fancy: not plain or simple

Visualize

What do you picture in your mind when Ant creeps onto the tablecloth, crouches down, and covers his face? What do you think he's feeling?

"Wait!" yells Ladybug. "Another family is coming! Maybe they'll be different."

Ant just sighs.

The mother places a tablecloth on the ground, and the family plops on it. Then she opens a big basket of yummy-smelling food.

Ladybug flies onto the boy's knee to introduce herself. The family *oohs* and *aahs* when they see her **fancy** shell.

Ladybug waves to Ant and shouts, "Come on! These people are lovely!"

Reluctantly, Ant creeps up onto the tablecloth. The boy sees Ant and shouts, "It's an ant!"

Ant crouches down and covers his face, fearing he would be smooshed. Instead, the boy carefully picks up Ant and shows him to his parents.

"This is my favorite insect," says the boy. "Did you know that ants are good for the earth? They tunnel inside the **soil**, bringing air with them. This is good for the plants because their roots need air."

Ant smiles.

"There's something else, too," says the father. "They take our trash and all kinds of **discarded** food inside the soil. That makes the soil richer for plants."

By this time, Ant is strutting around on the boy's hand.

"Can I take the ant and ladybug home for my insect collection?" the boy asks.

Ladybug is sad. She doesn't want to leave her home in the grass.

"Oh no," says the boy's mother. "These bugs still have important jobs to do."

So Ant and Ladybug decide it is time to leave.

"Where are you going?" asks Ant.

"I'm heading to the garden so I can eat those nasty pests off the plants. What about you?" says Ladybug.

"I've got important digging to do," says Ant. And off he proudly marches.

soil: top layer of dirt on the ground

discarded: thrown away

Point of View

How does Ant's point of view about people change at the end of the story?

Genre

Fantasy: A fantasy is a made-up story that has characters, settings, or other elements that could not exist in real life. A fantasy often has dialogue.

Make and Confirm Predictions

Think Aloud

Remember that we make predictions as we read. To help us, we can think about what the characters say. It is Bunny's birthday. He says, "We are going to make a carrot cake for my birthday." I predict that his friends will all help make Bunny's carrot cake. What do you predict will happen next? Let's keep reading and check to see if our predictions are correct.

announces: makes something known to everyone around you

Bunny's Big Birthday

Today is Bunny's big birthday, and he wants to throw a special party. He blows up balloons. He makes a banner. But something is missing.

"I know. A cake!" says Bunny. But he doesn't want to make the cake all by himself. So Bunny asks his friends Mouse, Bee, and Squirrel to come over and help.

"We are going to make a carrot cake for my birthday," Bunny **announces**.

"But I don't eat carrots, I eat cheese," says Mouse.

"And I eat honey," says Bee.

"And I eat nuts," says Squirrel.

"But I eat carrots, and it's *my* birthday!" says Bunny.

Then he gets an idea. "Let's make muffins instead of one **whole** cake. We can each have the kind of muffin we want. We can make a carrot muffin, a cheese muffin, a honey muffin, *and* a nut muffin!"

"Yum!" says Mouse, Bee, and Squirrel. And they all race to the grocery store.

Back at Bunny's house, the friends gather in the kitchen and dump all the **ingredients** on the table.

"Let's get to work," says Bunny.

First, they make the batter with eggs, flour, and milk. Then they stir in the rest of the ingredients and bake the muffins. But there's a problem. Everything is all mixed up!

"Ew!" says Bunny. "Mouse's cheese is in my carrot muffin!"

"Gross!" says Mouse. "Bee's honey is in my cheese muffin!"

"Ick!" says Bee. "Squirrel's nuts are in my honey muffin!"

"Yuck!" says Squirrel. "Bunny's carrots are in my nut muffin!"

whole: in one piece

ingredients: things used to make food

Point of View

Think Aloud

Remember that a character's point of view is the way he or she thinks or feels. Bunny says, "We can each have the kind of muffin we want." This tells me Bunny's point of view about his friends. Let's think more about point of view as we continue reading.

Make and Confirm Predictions

Think Aloud

I need to correct my prediction because I was wrong about Bunny's friends helping him make a cake. They are making muffins instead. Now I predict that after a rough start, Bunny and his friends will figure out how to organize their ingredients. Let's keep reading to see if my new prediction is correct. Was your prediction correct? What do you predict will happen next?

trouble: problems or difficulties

trudge: walk slowly because you are working hard

batch: one set of something you are baking

Point of View
How is Bunny's point of view about his birthday different now?

Make and Confirm Predictions

Think Aloud

My prediction was correct! Bunny says, "I think we should sort everything first." I will read to see what happens next.

Fantasy
How do you know this story is a fantasy?

"Oh my," says Bunny. "These muffins are turning out to be a lot of **trouble**. This is not a very good birthday. We need new ingredients." So they all **trudge** back to the grocery store to buy what they need.

When they return to Bunny's kitchen, the friends try again. First they make the batter with eggs, flour, and milk. They are about to stir in the rest of the ingredients when Bunny says, "Stop! We don't want this **batch** of muffins to turn out like the last one. I think we should sort everything first."

"Yes," says Mouse. "I will take all the cheese."

"Good idea," says Bee. "I will take all the honey."

"Of course," says Squirrel. "I will take all the nuts."

"Great!" says Bunny. "Now all the carrots are left for me. Let's get cooking!"

So this time, Bunny's friends mix a little batter in their own bowls with their favorite food. Then they put the muffins in the oven to bake.

Soon, wonderful smells **drift** out of the oven. The muffins are ready, and it's time to start the party. Everyone gathers around the table.

"Mmm," says Mouse. "This cheese muffin looks delicious!"

"Wow," says Bee. "This honey muffin looks tasty!"

"Ooh," says Squirrel. "This nut muffin looks yummy!"

"Yay!" says Bunny. "This birthday isn't so bad after all." And he blows out the candles on his carrot muffin. His wish for a special party has already come true!

drift: moves through the air

Point of View
How do you know Bunny's point of view about his birthday has changed?

Make and Confirm Predictions
Have partners confirm the predictions they made.

casts: gives off

stamps: puts his foot on the ground with great force

Fantasy

How do we know that this is a fantasy story?

Plot: Cause and Effect

Think Aloud

We have learned that a cause is what makes something happen, and an effect is the event that happens. I read that Mama tells Little Cricket that he can stay up late. This is the cause. "Little Cricket dances on his tiny legs" is the effect. Let's look for other causes and effects as I continue reading.

Little Cricket Stays Up Late

The sky is dark, and the moon **casts** a soft light over the field. Little Cricket sings his song alongside Mama Cricket.

"Mama," he says, "can I stay up late? I want to see the sun!"

"No, Little Cricket," says Mama. "You need your rest during the day. It's our job to sing at night."

Little Cricket **stamps** his tiny foot. "But I'm tired of singing all night in the dark," he says.

"It's not dark," says Mama. "The moonlight is lovely."

"Moonlight is boring," says Little Cricket. "I want to see the sun!"

"Very well, Little Cricket," says Mama. "You can stay up late. You will see the sun." And Little Cricket dances on his tiny legs.

When the sun comes up, Little Cricket wants to go **exploring**.

"Are you sure you wouldn't rather stay in our field?" asks Mama.

"No!" says Little Cricket as he **stretched** his wings, ready to go. "The sun is bright. There is so much to see! You **leaped** in the sunlight when you were my age, didn't you?" And he pulls Mama along with his tiny arm. Suddenly, they hear a loud "CAW, CAW!"

"Watch out!" cries Mama. She pulls Little Cricket back into the grass just in time to escape an **enormous** bird. "The sun *is* bright, and there *is* a lot to see," she says. "But that makes it easy for hungry birds to see you, too."

Little Cricket is still shaking as he peeks out at the enormous bird. "I guess you're right," says Little Cricket. And he frowns a tiny frown.

exploring: traveling around and discovering new things

stretched: extended or pulled a part of the body

leaped: jumped

enormous: very big

Make and Confirm Predictions

Think Aloud

I predict that because the hungry bird scared Little Cricket, he will go back to his field where it's safe. What is your prediction? Let's keep reading to see if our predictions are correct.

Think Aloud

I need to correct my prediction because I was wrong about Little Cricket going back to his field. Now I will use what I think and what has happened in the story so far to make a new prediction. I predict that Little Cricket will go home soon because he will be tired from all of his adventures. Let's keep reading to see if my new prediction is correct. Was your prediction correct? If so, continue making predictions. If not, make a new prediction, and check it as we continue reading.

escape: get away from something

Little Cricket and Mama Cricket come out of their field and walk along the street. Soon they come to a playground. "It must be fun to play here all day in the sun," says Little Cricket. "There is so much to do!"

"Wouldn't you like to go play by the big oak tree in our field?" asks Mama.

"No," says Little Cricket. "I want to explore this playground."

Suddenly, they hear a loud "BAM, BAM, BAM!"

"Watch out!" cries Mama. She pulls Little Cricket away just in time to **escape** a big, bouncing ball and the kids running after it. "Kids *do* play here all day in the sun," she says. "There *is* a lot to do. But kids' toys are a lot bigger than you."

Little Cricket and Mama go back to the sidewalk, where there are no more balls and no more kids.

"I guess you're right," says Little Cricket. "I didn't think about kids and their bouncing toys." And he hangs his tiny head.

Little Cricket and Mama Cricket keep on walking. As they go along, Little Cricket sees the sun get higher and brighter in the sky. "It must be nice to be out in the sun every day," says Little Cricket. "It is so warm!"

But then suddenly Mama Cricket hears a loud "PHEW!"

"What is it?" cries Mama. She turns to see Little Cricket slump against the side of a tree.

"The sun *is* warm," says Little Cricket. "Maybe *too* warm!" And he wipes his tiny brow.

"Come, Little Cricket," says Mama. "Let's go home."

Back in the field, the sun is setting. As the sky darkens and the moon comes up, Mama Cricket asks, "Did you like the sun?"

"Not as much as I thought I would," says Little Cricket. "I guess you were right. The moonlight *is* lovely!"

Little Cricket begins to sing alongside Mama Cricket. In the cool night air, he sings his best song ever. And he smiles a big, big smile.

Plot: Cause and Effect

We read what Little Cricket does as the sun gets higher and brighter in the sky. What is the cause, and what is the effect?

Make and Confirm Predictions

Think Aloud

My prediction was correct! Little Cricket goes home. I will read to see what happens next.

Make and Confirm Predictions

Have partners confirm the predictions they made.

The Schools of Critter Creek

In the tiny town of **Critter** Creek, there have always been two schools. And the two schools are as different as can be.

Everything at Elm School is cuddly and soft. The students sing soft lullabies. They play a gentle balloon toss. They read quiet poems in quiet whispers just like this.

Everything at Oak School is hard and loud. The students sing loud rock music. They play **rowdy** baseball with hard bats. They read exciting books in booming voices **JUST LIKE THIS!**

It has always been this way, as long as anyone can remember.

But Sally Squirrel has a problem. She goes to Elm School, but she **secretly** wants to go to Oak School.

She is tired of being soft and cuddly all the time.

She wants to learn something different.

At the very same time, Paco Porcupine has a problem. He goes to Oak School, but wishes he could go to Elm School.

He is tired of being hard and loud all the time.

He wants to learn something different, too.

So one day, they **demand** to switch schools.

"We want to try it, just for one day," Sally and Paco each **plead** with their teachers.

So their teachers say okay, just for one day.

Fantasy
What does Sally do that could not happen in real life?

Theme

Think Aloud

The theme of a story is the big idea or message. As I read, I look for clues that help me understand the message the author wants to share. Sally Squirrel and Paco Porcupine both demand to switch schools. They want to learn something different. I think this is a clue that will help me identify the theme. Let's find more clues as I continue to read.

Reread

Remember to ask me to reread any parts of the text that you don't understand.

booming: very loud and low

Theme

(Think Aloud)

I found another clue that helps me understand the message the author wants to share. Paco is the greatest at singing soft lullabies, and he loves playing with the balloon. Sally is a rock star playing rock music, and loves playing baseball with hard bats. Think about these clues as we continue to read.

Well, that one day finally comes.

Paco is the greatest at singing soft lullabies. He loves playing with the balloon. And he is the best at reading quiet poems in quiet whispers just like this.

And Sally is a rock star playing rock music. She loves playing baseball with hard bats. And she gets a gold star for reading an exciting book in a **booming** voice JUST LIKE THIS!

Both Sally and Paco have the best day either one can remember.

"Just because you go to Elm School, doesn't mean you only like soft and cuddly things," says Sally to her friends.

"Just because you go to Oak School, doesn't mean you don't have a soft side," says Paco to his friends.

Then all their friends wanted to try different things, too.

"I'd like to play in the soft sand pit," says Cassie Cat.

"And I'd like to try a rowdy game of dodge ball," says Randy Raccoon.

So the teachers and students from both schools realize they have an **emergency** on their hands. Something has to change! So they get together and decide to build a bridge between the two schools to become one big school. The teachers like this idea because then students from both schools can work together on all of their projects and activities. And all the critters agree that this school can be the best school in the land. And it is!

emergency: a sudden need for fast action

Theme
Think about the clues we've found as we read the story. What message does the author want to share?

meadow: flat, grassy land

Drama

What makes this a drama?

Reread

(Think Aloud)

Remember that we can reread text that we don't understand. I'm not sure why Birch Seed said, "Twinsies!" I reread a few lines and realized that Pine Seed calls them "Twin seeds." If you say that quickly, it sounds like Twinsies! Listen as I continue reading. If you don't understand something, ask me to stop and reread some of the text.

Twinsies

Cast: Narrator   Birch Seed   Pine Seed

Setting: a beautiful meadow

Narrator: Once upon a **meadow**, two little seeds landed in the dirt right next to each other. And they both said:

Birch Seed: Hello, neighbor!

Pine Seed: Hello, neighbor!

Narrator: These seeds looked and sounded a lot alike. Best of all, they enjoyed a lot of the same things.

Birch Seed: Do you like sunbathing? I *love* sunbathing!

Pine Seed: *I* love sunbathing, too! And singing in the rain! And blue jays and butterflies!

Birch Seed: *Me,* too! We're *so* alike!

Pine Seed: Twin seeds!

Birch Seed: Twinsies! (*giggle*)

Narrator: Day after day, the two seeds grew up together. They sprouted on the same morning.

Birch Seed: I'm a tiny sprout!

Pine Seed: I'm a tiny sprout, too!

Narrator: They took root the same week.

Birch Seed: My roots are growing!

Pine Seed: My roots are growing, too!

Narrator: They grew their branches together.

Birch Seed: Branch!

Pine Seed: Branch!

Birch Seed: Branch Branch!

Pine Seed: Branch Branch!

Both Seeds: Twinsies! (*giggle*)

Narrator: But then something important happened that was *not* the same.

Birch Seed: I'm growing leaves!

Pine Seed: I'm growing needles!

Plot: Sequence

Think Aloud

Remember that sequence is the order that events happen, and the events are the plot of the story. I learned that after the seeds grew branches, Birch Seed started growing leaves and Pine Seed started growing needles. Let's keep reading to find out what happens next.

Reread

Remember to ask me to reread any parts of the text that you don't understand.

suddenly: very quickly

lovely: beautiful

Birch Seed: My bark is turning white!

Pine Seed: My bark is brown!

Narrator: Suddenly they were not the same—at all.

Birch Seed: But we are supposed to be Twinsies!

Pine Seed: Yes, Twinsies!

Narrator: The more time passed, the more different they became.

Birch Seed: You can call me "Birch."

Pine Seed: You can call me "Pine."

Birch Seed: Fine.

Pine Seed: Fine.

Narrator: And the less like Twinsies they felt.

Birch Seed: *(to himself)* Just look at Pine with all those lovely pine cones. I don't have pine cones like that.

Pine Seed: *(to herself)* Just look at Birch with those beautiful leaves. I don't have leaves like that.

Plot: Sequence

What happens after the seeds agree to call each other by their names?

Narrator: The two old friends had never felt so different and so **miserable**. But then it started to rain.

Birch Seed: Sing!

Pine Seed: Sing!

Birch Seed: Sing!

Pine Seed: Sing!

Both Seeds: Sing sing sing sinnnnnnnng! (*giggle*)

Narrator: The rain stopped and the sun came out.

Birch Seed: I forgot how much we love singing in the rain. And blue jays!

Pine Seed: And sunbathing. And butterflies!

Birch Seed: We love *all* the same things.

Pine Seed: You know, just because we **discovered** that we don't *look* the same, doesn't mean we're *not* a lot alike.

Birch Seed: It's who we are, and what we love.

Pine Seed: You know what I love? Being best friends with you.

Birch Seed: Not only friends, Twinsies!

Narrator: And the two trees lived happily ever after.

miserable: very unhappy

Plot: Sequence
What happens while it rains? Why is this event important to understanding the plot of the play?

discovered: found out

Little Red Riding Hood

Once upon a time, there was a little girl who lived in a village with her mother. The little girl always wore a red cloak with a hood, so everyone called her Little Red Riding Hood.

One day, her mother said to her, "Grandmother is not feeling well, dear. Deliver this basket of bread and cheese to her to make her feel better. Do not **stray** or talk to strangers on the way."

"I won't, Mother," said Little Red Riding Hood. And off she went.

2

Grandmother lived in the woods, not far from the village. As Little Red Riding Hood was walking there, she met a wolf.

"Good morning," said the wolf. "Where are you going?"

"I am taking this basket to Grandmother."

"And where does she live?" asked the wolf.

"Her house is on the path, under three big oak trees," said Little Red Riding Hood.

The wolf thought, "This girl would make a mighty fine snack. But if I am **clever**, I can **feast** on the grandmother, too."

They walked along together for a while. Then the wolf said, "Look at all the pretty wildflowers. Perhaps Grandmother would like some."

"Yes, Grandmother likes flowers very much," thought Little Red Riding Hood. So she picked one, and then another, wandering farther and farther from the path.

clever: smart

feast: eat

Folktale:
What does the wolf do that tells you this is a folktale?

Make and Confirm Predictions

Think Aloud

Remember that we can make predictions using our thoughts about what will happen and then read on to see if we were correct. I predict that Little Red Riding Hood will get lost because she is picking flowers and is wandering far from the path. What is your prediction? Let's keep reading to see if our predictions are correct.

dainty: small and pretty

Make and Confirm Predictions

Think Aloud

I need to correct my prediction because I was wrong about Little Red Riding Hood getting lost. Now I will use what I think and what has happened in the story so far to predict that the wolf will eat Little Red Riding Hood too. Let's keep reading to see if my new prediction is correct.

Was your prediction correct? If so, continue making predictions. If not, make a new prediction, and check it as we continue reading.

While Little Red Riding Hood was busy picking flowers, the wolf ran to Grandmother's cottage and knocked on the door.

"Who's there?" called Grandmother.

"Little Red Riding Hood," said the wolf, in a **dainty** voice. "I've brought you some bread and cheese. Please open the door!"

"I am too weak to get up," called Grandmother. "Just come in."

The wolf entered the cottage and ate up Grandmother. Then he put on her nightgown and nightcap, got into bed, and pulled up the covers.

When Little Red Riding Hood got to Grandmother's cottage, she was surprised to see the door standing open. She was even more surprised at how strange Grandmother looked.

"Grandmother, what big ears you have," said Little Red Riding Hood.

"All the better to hear you with, my dear."

"Grandmother, what big eyes you have."

"All the better to see you with, my dear."

"Grandmother, what big teeth you have."

"All the better to EAT you with," said the wolf.

At that, he jumped out of bed and swallowed poor Little Red Riding Hood in one gulp. Then he went back to bed and was soon snoring loudly.

A hunter walking past the house heard a noise. "How loudly Old Grandmother is snoring. I must see if there is anything the matter with her." He went in and saw the wolf lying on Grandmother's bed. Suddenly, he **realized** that the wolf had swallowed her whole! "Maybe I can save her," he thought.

Now the wolf was sleeping very deeply, so the hunter slowly and carefully opened his jaws as wide as could be to see if there was anyone inside.

Out jumped Little Red Riding Hood, followed by Grandmother.

And what about the wolf? The hunter took him away and made sure that he would never bother anyone again.

Make and Confirm Predictions

(Think Aloud)

My prediction was correct! The wolf does eat Little Red Riding Hood. I will read to see what happens next.

realized: understood

Plot: Cause and Effect
We read what the hunter does. What is the cause and what is the effect?

Make and Confirm Predictions
Have partners confirm the predictions they made.

How Leopard Got Its Spots

Long ago and far away, many animals **roamed** the sandy desert. You could spot Zebra, Giraffe, and lots more. All the animals were shades of brown. Dark brown. Light brown. But none was as sandy-brown as the sandy-brown Leopard. When he walked on the sand or rested on the sandy rocks, it was as if he was **invisible**. No one could see him. Can you?

"I cannot spot the hungry Leopard," cried Zebra. "I cannot see his sharp teeth or pointy claws," cried Giraffe. "If we don't leave the desert, surely Leopard will gobble us up," they both moaned. So Giraffe and Zebra headed for the grasslands far away.

"Where have all the zebras and giraffes gone?" asked the **frustrated** Leopard one day as he traveled across the desert in search of his next meal. Nearby a man sat underneath a giant tree.

"They have all run away to the grasslands," he said. "If you want food, you must go there too. I will take you."

So Leopard and the man walked through the scorching heat of the desert until they arrived at the grasslands. The sandy-brown Leopard stood out like a bright flower in the shadows of the green grassy grasses in which he was trying to hide.

Leopard looked around, but all he could see were trees and tall grass.

"But where are Zebra and Giraffe?" asked Leopard. "I smell them, but I do not see them. How can that be?"

frustrated: felt angry or upset because you couldn't do something you wanted to do

Ask and Answer Questions

Think Aloud

Asking questions about the story can help us understand what is happening. I wonder why Leopard cannot see Zebra and Giraffe. I will continue reading to see if my question is answered. As I read, think of questions you have and then listen for the answers.

special: important

blotches: large spots

Ask and Answer Questions

(Think Aloud)

I noticed the answer to my question. In the story, Giraffe and Zebra have changed their fur. Zebra now has black and white stripes, and Giraffe has blotches. They blend in with the grass and trees, which is why Leopard can't see them. Remember to continue thinking about answers to your own questions.

Plot: Sequence

What happens next, after Leopard realizes that Zebra can blend in with the tall grasses, and Giraffe can blend in with the trees?

"It is a **special** trick," said the man. "Look closely. Giraffe and Zebra have changed their fur."

"What?" asked Leopard. He looked and looked but couldn't see them.

"Zebra now has black and white stripy stripes," the man said.

"But why?" asked Leopard.

"So he can blend into the tall grasses. You can smell him, but you can't find him. And Giraffe has done the same. Her hair is now covered in blotchy **blotches**, so she blends in with the trees."

"Oh, no," cried Leopard. "What will I do?"

"I have an idea," said the man.

The man poured some black ink into a wooden bowl, dipped his fingertips in, and made dots all over Leopard's body. Over and over.

"Spots, spots, and more spots," **exclaimed** Leopard looking at his new fur. "What are all these spots for?"

"Now you too can blend in with the shadows of the grasses and rocks and trees," said the man. "You can sneak up on Zebra and Giraffe, and they'll never know. You'll be the most feared hunter in all the grasslands."

And so he was. That, my dear listeners, is how the **splendid** leopard got its spots.

Plot: Sequence
What is the last event in the story?

Folktale
What does this folktale try to explain?

exclaimed: cried out with strong feelings

splendid: wonderful

Genre

Folktale: A folktale is a story that was handed down orally from one generation to the next.

Folktale

How do you know this is a folktale?

crowded: filled with too many people and things

Character, Setting, and Events

(Think Aloud)

Remember that thinking about the events can help us understand the story. One event is that Sara got upset with the mess and told Sam to go to the wise man for help. Listen for other events, information about the characters, and descriptions of the setting as I continue reading.

Now Things Are Worse!

Long ago, Sam and his wife, Sara, lived in a tiny cottage. Each day, they baked bread to sell. But Sam and Sara had a big problem. They lived with their six children, Sam's parents, and a dog and cat.

The cottage was always noisy, **crowded**, and messy. The children played, argued, and left their clothes on the floor. The grownups worked, shouted, and left pots on the stove. The dog and cat barked and meowed, and they made muddy tracks.

One day, Sara got upset. "I can't stand this mess anymore!" she said. "We can't bake our bread! Go to the wise man, Sam. He will help us."

So Sam went to see the wise man. "My wife and I need your help," he said. "We live in a tiny cottage with our six children, my parents, and a dog and cat. We are miserable. We can hardly get our work done!"

The wise man nodded and tugged on his beard. Then he asked, "Do you have any animals outside?"

"Oh, yes!" said Sam. "We have three chickens, a goat, and a cow."

"Bring the chickens inside the cottage to live with you," said the wise man.

Sam thought this was very strange advice. But he did it.

The chickens clucked day and night. They flapped their wings. Their feathers flew everywhere.

Sam and Sara did their best to **support** each other and their family. But soon, they couldn't stand it any longer.

support: give help to

Make and Confirm Predictions

Think Aloud

Remember that we can make predictions and then read to see if we were correct. Sam told the wise man why he and his wife are unhappy. I predict the wise man will tell Sam to build a new house or make his house bigger. What do you predict will happen? I'll read on to see if our predictions are correct.

Make and Confirm Predictions

Think Aloud

My prediction was not correct. The wise man told Sam to bring the chickens inside, not to build a bigger house. My next prediction is that Sam will go back to the wise man to ask for help. Was your prediction correct?

possessions: things owned

Make and Confirm Predictions

Think Aloud

My prediction about Sam returning to the wise man was correct. Let's make a new prediction. Look at the illustration. Think about the characters. What do you think will happen?

Character, Setting, and Events

Why is the wise man an important character? Why do you think Sam did what the wise man said to do?

So Sam returned to the wise man. "Wise man," said Sam, "I brought the chickens into our home. But now things are worse! We can't sleep with the noise. There are feathers in the bread!"

The wise man said, "Bring the goat inside to live with you."

"How will that solve our problem?" thought Sam. But he did it.

The goat bleated day and night. It ran around and chewed up the family's **possessions**. And the chickens continued to cluck, flap, and spread feathers everywhere.

Soon, Sam returned to the wise man. "I did as you said and brought the goat into our home," said Sam. "But now things are worse! The goat eats all our things! It bleats loudly and runs wild! The chickens are still noisy and messy, too."

The wise man said, "Bring the cow inside to live with you."

"We cannot live with a cow!" thought Sam. But he did it.

The cow mooed day and night. It crashed into chairs. The goat continued to bleat and chew and run wild. The chickens continued to cluck and flap and spread feathers everywhere. The cottage was a **disgusting** mess and noisier than ever! After a few days, Sam and Sara couldn't stand it. So Sam returned to the wise man.

"Wise man," said Sam, "I brought the cow into our home. But now things are even worse! We can't live with a cow, a goat, and chickens! It is too crowded!"

"You are absolutely right!" said the wise man. "Take all the animals out of your home."

So Sam did it. With all the animals out, the cottage seemed quiet, clean, and **cozy**. Sam and Sara were able to bake their bread. The children played nicely together. The grandparents were able to read and eat in peace.

Sara gave the wise man some of their delicious bread. "How can we ever thank you?" she said. "You have made life sweet for us!"

disgusting: so gross to look at, smell, or taste that you feel a little sick

cozy: comfortable and warm

Character, Setting, and Events
How did the cottage change from the beginning of the story to the end?

Make and Confirm Predictions
Ask partners to confirm the predictions they made.

Fairy Tale

How can you tell that this story is a fairy tale?

special: better than others

Key Details

Think Aloud

We look for important information, or key details, when we read a story. Key details help us understand what happens. I just read that Jack's mother threw the beans out the window. I think this is a key detail. Let's look for more key details as we continue reading.

Jack and the Beanstalk

A long time ago, a boy named Jack lived with his mother in a tiny cottage on a small farm. Jack and his mother were very poor. They had barely enough money for food.

One day, his mother asked Jack to sell their cow at the market in town. So Jack took the cow to market, where he met a farmer.

"Sell me your cow for these beans," said the farmer.

"I cannot sell our cow for beans!" replied Jack.

"These are **special** beans," said the farmer. "Plant them, and stalks will grow to the sky!"

So Jack sold the cow for the beans. However, when he returned home, his mother was furious and tossed the beans out the window.

The next morning, Jack woke up and looked out the window. He saw an enormous beanstalk that reached high into the sky, past the clouds!

He wondered what would happen if he climbed up the beanstalk. So he started climbing from one leaf to another. Up, up, up.

When he finally got to the top, he saw a **huge** house with a huge window and a huge door. He looked in the window. Two giants, a man and a woman, were eating breakfast at a huge table. The man sniffed the air and said,

"Fee-fum-fo-fee, someone's here with you and me!"

"**Nonsense**," said his wife. Then they fell asleep next to their bowls of porridge.

Jack looked around the large kitchen. There were many bags of gold. One was on the table by the sleeping giants.

Quietly, Jack crept into the kitchen and took one bag of gold. Without waiting a moment, he climbed down the beanstalk as fast as he could. When his mother saw the gold, she was thrilled.

huge: very big

nonsense: foolish or untrue words

Reread

Think Aloud

Remember that we can go back and reread the text if we don't understand something. I don't understand why Jack took the bag of gold. When I reread the text on the previous page, it said that Jack and his mother were very poor. Listen as I continue reading. If you don't understand something, ask me to stop and reread some of the text.

Reread

Remember to ask me to reread any parts of the text that you don't understand.

spent: used all of the money by buying things

Key Details

What happened when Jack went up the beanstalk the second time? Why is it important?

After a while, Jack and his mother **spent** all the gold. So it was decided that Jack would climb the beanstalk again. This time, when he got to the top and looked in their window, he saw the giants with a hen.

The man commanded, "Lay!" and the hen laid a golden egg!

Jack couldn't believe it! First gold and now a hen that laid golden eggs!

All of the sudden, the man sniffed the air and said,

"Fee-fum-fo-fee, someone's here with you and me!"

"Nonsense," said his wife. Then they quickly fell into a deep sleep.

Quietly, Jack tiptoed over to the hen, gently took her in his arms, and climbed down the beanstalk. His mother loved the hen that laid golden eggs!

More time passed, and Jack finally **returned** to the giants' house. He was able to climb quickly up the beanstalk by now.

returned: went back

This time, the giants had a golden harp on the table in front of them. When the woman demanded, "Sing!" the harp sang beautifully. Again they fell into a deep sleep. While they napped, Jack snuck in the house and took the harp. However, this time, the giant man and his wife woke up! They looked around and saw Jack. Then the giant man roared,

"Fee-fum-fo-fee, someone's here with you and me!"

With the harp clutched in his arms, Jack raced down the beanstalk. The giant followed, but Jack was faster. When he got home, Jack took his ax and chopped down the beanstalk. The giant crashed down through the earth and was never seen again!

Jack and his mother lived happily ever after, selling golden eggs and listening to their harp play beautiful music.

Key Details
What is the most important thing that happened at the end of the story? Why is it a key detail?

Key Details

Think Aloud

We look for key details as we read and listen to nursery rhymes. Key details give important information. When I read the beginning of the nursery rhyme, a key detail is the speaker counts "one, two." Then in the next line she counts "three, four." These are key details that tell me that this is a counting rhyme. Let's look for other key details as we read.

shut: close

1, 2, Buckle My Shoe

1, 2,

Buckle my shoe.

3, 4,

Shut the door.

5, 6,

Pick up sticks.

7, 8,

Lay them **straight**.

9, 10,

Let's count again!

Nursery Rhyme
Tell how you know this is a nursery rhyme.

straight: without a bend or a curve

Key Details
What important detail do you learn at the end of the nursery rhyme?

Mary Had a Little Lamb

sure: certain to happen

Mary had a little lamb, little lamb,
Little lamb,

Mary had a little lamb
Whose fleece was white as snow.

And everywhere that Mary went
Mary went, Mary went,

Everywhere that Mary went
The lamb was **sure** to go.

Visualize

Think Aloud

Remember that as we read, we can visualize, or make a picture in our minds, of what is happening. I read that the lamb followed Mary everywhere she went. I picture in my mind the lamb following Mary all around the farm and into her house! This tells me more about how much the lamb loves to be with Mary. Continue to visualize as I read more of the nursery rhyme.

He followed her to school one day,
School one day, school one day,

He **followed** her to school one day,
Which was against the **rules**.

It made the children laugh and play,
Laugh and play, laugh and play,

It made the children laugh and play
To see a lamb at school.

followed: went behind someone

rules: ideas about what you can and cannot do

Visualize

What picture do you have in your mind of children playing with the lamb at school? What does this tell you about how the children feel about the lamb?

Poetry

What are two words in this poem that rhyme?

Key Details

Think Aloud

Key details in the words and illustrations can help us understand a poem. The text describes what the goldfish cannot do, and the illustration shows the boy playing with his ball because he can't play with the fish. These key details tell us more about the relationship between the boy and his fish.

fetch: go get and bring back

leap: jump

slimy: sticky and slippery

My Goldfish

My goldfish cannot **fetch** a ball.

She doesn't come when I call.

She won't curl up with me to sleep.

When I get home, she doesn't **leap**.

She's tiny, **slimy**, and always wet.

So what makes her the nicest pet?

Maybe it's how she swims to me,

When I look in just to see.

So there we are just the two of us.

Eye to eye and nose to nose.

For a moment I know what
a goldfish knows.

And my heart can go where
a goldfish goes.

Key Details
*The text and
illustration describe the
boy putting his face up
to the fish bowl. What
details tell you why the
boy does this?*

Who Can?

Poetry

What words in this poem repeat? Why does the author use repeated words?

Visualize

Think Aloud

The author tells us that the cat can sleep, hide, and curl up. When I close my eyes, I can see the cat hiding in a bowl and curling up in a drawer. This helps me understand the different and interesting things the cat can do. Let's continue to visualize as we read more of the poem.

ledge: a shelf sticking out from a wall

Who can . . .
Sleep on a book?
Hide in bowl?
Curl up in a drawer?
My cat can do that!

Who can . . .
Jump to a **ledge**?
Climb a curtain?
Then land on my chair?
My cat can do that!

Who can . . .
Purr in my lap?
Nuzzle my nose?
Make me feel glad?
My cat can do that.
I love, love, love my cat!

nuzzle: lie close and rub

Visualize

Can you picture the cat in the girl's lap? What is the cat doing? How does this make the girl feel?

Genre

Poetry: Poetry is a kind of writing that has short lines and often has rhyme and repetition.

Key Details

Think Aloud

Key details in the words and illustrations can help us understand a poem. The text describes what the speaker is learning to do, including playing catch with a friend. The illustration shows two friends playing catch. These key details tell us more about what the speaker is learning to do.

sight: by looking

Things I'm Learning

I'm learning to play catch.

I play it with my friend.

Back and forth and back and forth

The fun will never end!

I also read more words.

I know those words by **sight**.

But I still love to hear my dad

Read books to me at night.

I used to get upset

If I didn't get my way.

But friends taught me how to **share**

And now we play all day.

I'm learning many things.

So many of them new.

There's nothing that can stop me now.

There's nothing I can't do!

share: use and enjoy something together

Key Details
What does the speaker learn when playing with friends?

Poetry
How do you know this selection is a poem?

Look at How I Grew

Stop and hop, lollipop.
There's so much I can do.
Spinning, **twirling**, jumping, running
Just to name a few.

Better **shake**, rattlesnake.
There's so much I can do.
Reading, writing, sharing
With a silly friend or two.

Out the door, dinosaur.
There's so much I can do.
Sitting, listening, talking
Every day to you and you.

twirling: turning in circles

shake: move quickly back and forth or up and down

Visualize

Think Aloud

We can visualize, or make pictures in our mind, as we read this poem. I read that the speaker can sit and talk with friends. I can picture friends having a fun time together. It helps me understand what the speaker has learned to do. Let's keep visualizing as we read.

Take care, polar bear
There's so much I can do.
Riding, swimming, spelling
Words like "rhino" or "kazoo."

See you later, alligator.
There's so much I can do.
I learned a lot in this long year.
Oh, look at how I **grew**!

Visualize
What do you picture in your mind when I read about the speaker going swimming?

grew: improved in some way

Genre

Informational Text: This genre tells about real people, places, things, or events by presenting facts and information about them.

Key Details

Think Aloud

This text helps us understand some important things about first grade. For example, it is important to cooperate. One way to cooperate is by sharing the work. This is a key detail because it tells us something we need to know about being a first grader. Listen for more key details as I read.

expected: believed someone will do something that is wanted

Work, Play, and Learn Together

Hooray! You're in first grade now. You probably have lots of questions about what first grade will be like: *Will I get along with others and make friends? What is* **expected** *of me? What if I feel scared or I don't know what to do?* If you've asked yourself questions like these, don't worry. Over time, you'll learn what you need to know! Meanwhile, here are ideas to help you get started.

Whenever you work or play as part of group, it's important to cooperate. Let's say you're working with a group on a science project or a mural. Each person works on *part* of the project or paints *part* of the mural.

2

Troels Graugaard/Getty Images

successful: reached a goal

pay attention: listen carefully to

directions: instructions that tell how to do something

Visualize

Think Aloud

Remember that when we visualize, we create pictures in our minds of what is happening in a text. Here it says that your class may have a list of rules, such as walking in the hallways. When I close my eyes, I can see children walking quietly down the hallway from one place to another, and it helps me understand why rules are an important part of school. Let's keep visualizing as I continue reading.

You share the work and when you're done, you end up with a terrific project or a big, beautiful painting. Cooperative kids know that by working well together and doing their part, everyone ends up being **successful**!

First-graders need to be responsible, too. What does that mean? Part of being responsible means you **pay attention** to your teacher and follow **directions**. If you're not sure what to do, raise your hand and let your teacher know. Teachers are happy to answer questions and explain things because they want you to understand and learn.

Another part of being responsible means following classroom rules. Maybe your class has a list of rules: keep your space neat and clean; return materials after using them; walk—never run—in the classroom and hallways; raise your hand when you have something to say. Why are rules important? They make your classroom a safe and friendly place to work, play, and learn together.

3

Visualize

What picture do you have in your mind of how you might act if you are sad about something?

Informational Text

How do you know this selection is informational text?

There may be times when you come to school feeling really happy or a little sad. Maybe you made a new friend in your neighborhood or found a toy that you thought was lost forever. So you walk into school feeling great! Maybe your pet is missing or you had a disagreement with a friend or someone in your family. You might go to school feeling sad. Happy and sad events like these can make your day in school either really good or a little sad.

There may also be times when something happens in the classroom that makes you feel sad. When these things happen, the best thing you can do is express your feelings. That means you tell others how you feel. When you hold sad feelings inside, they grow, which doesn't feel good. But when you share them with your teacher or classmates, you let them out and you feel much better!

Even classmates who are good friends can sometimes have problems. Maybe you feel left out of an activity or someone doesn't want to share a book. When kids aren't getting along, they may lose their temper and yell or even push each other. But yelling and pushing only hurt your feelings and make the problem worse! So the best thing to do is to sit down and discuss the problem together. Take turns talking and listening carefully to each other. When you're **wrong** about something, say you're sorry. That helps a lot! If you get stuck and can't solve a problem, ask your teacher to help you figure out what's fair.

Now that you've heard about some important ideas about working together and getting along, such as cooperating, being responsible, expressing yourself, and solving problems, you're ready to put them into practice. Keep them in mind as you do activities, and you'll have a great year in first grade!

Key Details
What is one thing you can do when you have a problem with a friend?

wrong: not right

asiseeit/E+/Getty Images

Genre

Informational Text:
This genre tells about real people, places, things, or events by presenting information and facts. Informational text can include photos to give information.

Informational Text

What topic in real life are you learning about?

Ask and Answer Questions

Think Aloud

Asking questions about the text can help us understand what is happening. I wonder how the pieces fit together to make a finished puzzle. I will continue reading to see if my question is answered. As I read, think of questions you have and then listen for the answers.

goal: something to achieve

Time with Friends

It's fun to do things with friends. You can learn from each other. For example, you can learn about different games and festivals from around the world.

Time for Teamwork

Do you like puzzles? Finding that just-right piece can be such fun! There are many different kinds of puzzles. One kind is called a tangram. Some people think the first tangram puzzles were played long ago and far away in China, a country in Asia.

Tangram puzzles are fun to do with a friend. You start with seven flat puzzle pieces, each with its own shape. The pieces are called tans. That's why the puzzle is called a tangram. The **goal** is to make a larger shape using these seven smaller pieces.

2

How do you get started? First, you start with a box of tans. Then you choose an outline of a larger shape you would like to work with. It can be an animal, like a cat or dragon, or an object, like a boat or house. Next, **arrange** the seven tans to fill in the larger shape. But remember, the tans cannot **overlap**. You and a friend will have to put on your thinking caps to finish these puzzles! Also, remember that sometimes there is more than one way to solve a tangram.

Look at the tans arranged in the square in the picture. Then look at the shape outlines. What animal and object do you see? Notice that all seven tans were used to complete each tangram.

You can also create tangrams of your own! You can arrange your seven tans in any way you want. Challenge your friends to create different designs!

Ask and Answer Questions

Think Aloud

I noticed the answer to my question. The text says that you look at an outline of a larger shape and then arrange the tans to fill it in. Remember to look for the answers to your own questions.

Key Details

Think Aloud

Key details can help us understand informational text. The text says that the seven tans cannot overlap. This is a key detail because it tells me something important about how to put together the tangram. Let's keep this key detail in mind as we continue reading.

arrange: put in a particular order or set up

overlap: to lay over something so that it's partly covered

Time to Play

Do you have fun playing outside? Do you have a favorite game to play with friends at the park? There is an outdoor game that you might not know, but that is very fun. It's called Pilolo. Pilolo is a game from Ghana, a country in Africa.

Pilolo is like tag and hide-and-seek combined into one game. One player hides sticks while you and all the other players cover your eyes. Don't peek! Remember, peeking is against the rules. You need to wait until the person hiding the sticks yells, "Ready, set, go!" That is when you can open your eyes and run around searching for the hidden sticks.

If you find a stick, carry it across the finish line as fast as you can. The first one across the finish line is the winner! Win or lose, Pilolo is a lot of fun. It is also a game that gives you good exercise. Where could you play Pilolo in your neighborhood?

Key Details

What is one way the friends work together to play Pilolo?

Time to Celebrate

Do you have a favorite festival or holiday? Does it include yummy food, fun games, or special **customs**? Many do! There is often a lot to prepare for big celebrations. And as they say, "many hands make light work." That means it's best when you and your friends work together to prepare for celebrations.

One popular festival is from India and Nepal, two countries in Asia. This festival is called Holi. The festival celebrates good spring **harvests**, saying farewell to winter, and enjoying the colors of spring. The most important event during the festival is the throwing of colored water and powder on friends and family. Why do people celebrate Holi this way?

Imagine all the beautiful flowers that pop up and bloom in spring—the season when so many colorful things start to grow. This throwing of colored water and powder represents, or stands for, the coming of spring with all its beautiful colors. Is this a holiday you would like to celebrate in your town? What other festivals and holidays do you celebrate each season with family and friends?

customs: ways of doing things followed by a group of people

harvests: the time of year when crops are gathered

PhotosIndia.com LLC/Alamy

Key Details
Look at the photograph. What key detail do you learn about Holi by looking at the photograph?

Informational Text:
This genre tells about real people, places, things, or events by presenting information and facts about them, and by using photos.

dash: run quickly

Informational Text

What makes this an informational text?

Key Details

Think Aloud

The text says that bones are important in helping our bodies move, and, in the photograph, I see the bones the girl uses to help her body move. These are key details because they tell me how our bodies move. Let's keep these key details in mind as we continue reading.

Let's Move!

Leap. Bounce. Dive. **Dash**. Your body likes to move and it can move in many fun ways. You use different body parts—feet, legs, arms, and hands—to help you move.

Do you like to kick a ball down a soccer field? Do you like to pedal a bike through the park? If you do, your feet play an important role in helping you move. How? Your feet are made up of bones. Bones are hard and white and found all over the inside of your body.

Imagine building a house out of sticks. The sticks are the house's structure. The sticks hold up the house. On top of the sticks, you can add a roof, doors and windows, furniture, and other things. Your bones make up the structure of your body. They are needed to hold it up. They also help your body move.

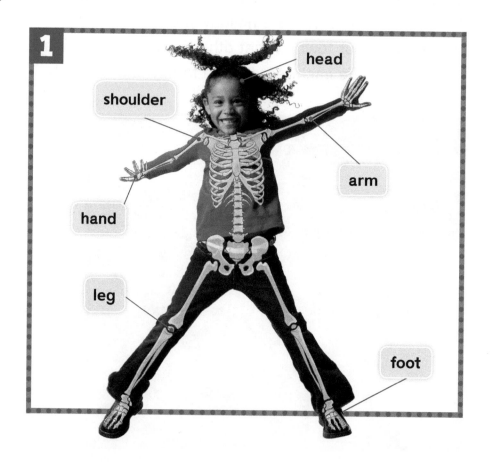

1

head

shoulder

arm

hand

leg

foot

2

Together, your bones make up what's called your skeleton. Your bones are **connected** by joints that allow your body to bend. Hold out your leg as straight as you can. Now bend it at the knee joint. Touch the knee. What you feel is a bone!

Do you like to run around during recess? Do you like to take **gigantic** leaps over puddles? If you do, your legs play an important role. You can use your legs to jump up and down, hop like a kangaroo, or walk down the hallway. Your legs can also help you run a race or flip like a gymnast.

You also use your legs to swim and play soccer. When you swim, you kick your legs to help you move through the water. During a soccer game, you use your legs to run down the field and kick a goal!

Look at these kids. How are they using their legs when they do ballet?

connected: joined together

gigantic: really big

Ask and Answer Questions

Think Aloud

Remember that asking questions about the text as we read can help us understand what is happening. I wonder why joints are important. I will continue reading to see if my question is answered. As I continue reading, think of questions you have and then listen for the answers.

Ask and Answer Questions

Think Aloud

I noticed the answer to my question. It says that my joints help my legs run, jump, and flip, and even kick. Remember to look for the answers to your own questions.

While your feet and legs help you move all day, so do your arms and hands. If you like to climb a tree or catch a ball, your hands play an important role. Your hands also come in "handy" when clapping for your favorite team.

Hands can be used for big movements like throwing a ball, or small movements like writing with a pencil. Inside your hands are many tiny bones. Together they help you **grip** objects. Look at the boy in the wheelchair. How is he using his hands? Why are they important in helping him move?

Look at your hands. Then think of all of the ways you use your hands every day, from holding a spoon or fork, to scratching your dog's belly, to fitting puzzle pieces together. Your hands are important tools.

grip: hold tightly

Key Details

What are some different ways that people use their hands?

When you play softball or baseball, your arms play an important role. You also use your arms to steer a bike, throw a frisbee, and play double Dutch with jump ropes. How do your arms have the **strength** to move in so many ways? Put your hand on the inside of your arm, right above the elbow. Now bend your arm. Do you feel something pop up a little bit? That's your muscle!

Your muscles sit on top of your bones. They are needed for you to lift, stretch, pull, and push. You have muscles all over your body. When you exercise, you make your muscles stronger. Stronger muscles help your body move better.

Look at these kids. How are they using their arms? What other body parts are they using to move?

Leap. Bounce. Dive. Dash. We learned that bones, joints, and muscles help our legs, hands, and other parts of our bodies move. Which parts of your body did you use to move today?

strength: being physically strong

Key Details
What happens when we have stronger muscles? Why is this a key detail?

Dream Pictures/The Image Bank/Getty Images

Genre

Informational Text:
This genre tells about real people, places, things, or events by presenting facts about them.

Ask and Answer Questions

Remember that we can ask questions while we read. Then we can look for the answers. I ask myself what a hobby is. I will keep reading to see if I can find an answer to my question. Listen as I read and think of your own questions.

Ask and Answer Questions

I see the answer to my question. A hobby is something you like to do, such as painting or playing a sport. Remember to look for the answers to your own questions.

express: show

What Do You Like to Do?

Do you have a hobby that you enjoy? I bet the answer is *yes*! Maybe you like to draw and paint pictures or play musical instruments. Maybe you enjoy doing experiments to figure out how things work. If you like to be active, then you're probably good at sports. All the things you like to do are part of what makes you the special person you are.

If you're someone who enjoys drawing and painting, then guess what—you're an artist! You might like to paint pictures of things in nature, like trees and flowers, or maybe you enjoy painting pictures of the people and pets you love. Some artists create pictures that **express** how they feel. They use color, lines, and shapes to show whether they feel happy or sad at that moment.

KidStock/Blend Images

2

Using different materials like crayons, chalk, paint, and markers make art interesting, too. And when you're done, you can hang your picture on the wall!

Do you spend lots of time making music or singing? If so, then you're a musician! Many musicians like to play in a band with others. A band plays music as a team, but at the same time everyone adds something special to the music with the instrument he or she plays. Music helps you understand that together, you can **create** something bigger and better than each of you could create alone. And best of all, music can make you happy and give you lots of energy!

create: make something

Key Details

Think Aloud

We know to look for key details, or important information, when we read an informational text. I read that in a band, everyone adds something special, even though a band plays music as a team. This is a key detail. Let's find more key details as we continue reading.

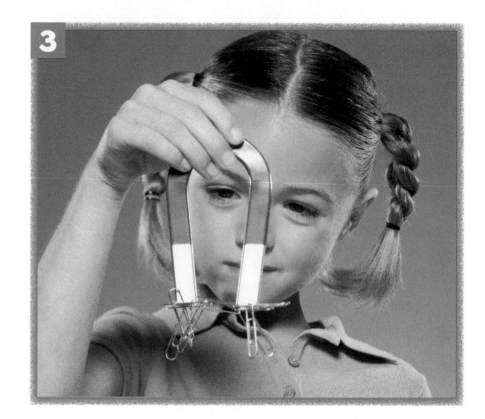

fascinated: very
interested in

Key Details

*What key detail helps
you know if you are a
scientist?*

If you often wonder about the things you see in nature
or are **fascinated** with how things work, then you can
call yourself a scientist! Kids who enjoy science as a
hobby ask lots of questions and then investigate to figure
out the answers.

For example, you might build a model of a volcano
to show why and how it erupts and then share what
you learned with your classmates. Or you might do
an experiment to find out why magnets attract some
objects and not others. Sometimes scientists work alone
and sometimes they work with others, but one thing is
true of all scientists—they're very curious about the world
around them!

Do you like to play sports with speed and **skill**? Then you're definitely an athlete! Playing sports is a great way to have fun and stay fit. If you play team sports, like baseball and soccer, you also learn how to get along with teammates and coaches and how important it is to follow the rules of the game.

Karate isn't a team sport, but it is popular and something many athletes enjoy. When you participate in karate, you learn how to be both physically fit and **focused** as you practice special kicking and punching movements. The more you practice, the faster and stronger you become!

So keep having hobbies, whatever they may be, because you will enjoy and learn from them for the rest of your life. And think about this—sometimes a special hobby that you love can end up leading to the career you choose when you grow up!

Informational Text

What real place are you learning about?

Main Topic and Key Details

Think Aloud

Remember that the main topic is what the selection is all about. The main topic of this selection is animals who live at a pond. On this page, I read that one pond animal, the turtle, swims in the pond. This is a key detail about an animal that lives at a pond. Let's look for other key details as we continue reading.

croak: deep sound made by a frog

species: group of related living things

Stephen Therres/Shutterstock.com

Animals at the Pond

Have you ever been to a pond? Did you feed the ducks while they splashed in the water? Did you hear a bullfrog **croak**?

How about a turtle? Did you spy a turtle sunning itself on a log or creeping onto the land? Maybe you saw a turtle swimming!

For these animals, ponds are home. Some live in the water, some live on the land, and a few live in both. Did you know that some ponds may have as many as 1,000 animal **species**? Let's meet a few and find out why the pond is a good place for them to live.

1

2

BUZZZ . . . Who is making that loud sound? A dragonfly! Dragonflies can look and sound like tiny airplanes as they zip and zoom up in the sky. So why do these high-flyers stick so close to the pond? That's where they lay their eggs.

Young dragonflies, which are called nymphs, live in the water until they are fully grown. When the nymphs crawl out of the water, they **shed** their skin, and become adults with wings.

Dragonflies eat just about any insect they can catch in flight. And, they have the biggest eyes of any bug. They can see in all directions and can even spot a tiny mosquito move almost anywhere in the pond!

shed: to fall off the body

Reread

Think Aloud

Remember that we can go back and reread the text if we don't understand something. I don't understand why dragonflies have such big eyes. Then I reread the last paragraph and read that the big eyes help them see other animals flying around the pond. Listen as I continue reading. If you don't understand something, ask me to stop and reread some of the text.

creatures: any living people or animals

Reread

Remember to ask me to reread any parts of the text that you don't understand.

Main Topic and Key Details

What key details do you learn about frogs that live in and around the pond?

Like dragonflies, frogs are special pond **creatures** because they live part of their lives in the water and part on land.

A mother frog lays eggs in the pond. After a few days, tadpoles come out of the eggs. The tadpoles have long tails and no legs. They have gills on their bodies like a fish. The gills help them to breathe under the water. Tadpoles eat algae, which are plants that grow in the water.

Slowly, the tadpoles grow legs and lungs. The lungs help them breathe air. Finally, the tadpoles lose their gills and tails and hop onto land as adult frogs.

Adult frogs can get their food without going into the water at all. They can sit on a lily pad and use their long tongues to catch a flying insect. Yum!

Everyone knows that ducks like to be in a pond. But have you ever seen a tall white bird with a long neck and long legs? This is an egret. An egret loves the pond and uses its long legs to wade in the **shallow** water. From there it can see what is happening below water. When an egret wants a meal, it can put its long neck into the water and snap up a fish.

Turtles, dragonflies, frogs, and egrets. These animals and many others call a pond home. Why? It's a good place to live!

shallow: not deep

Main Topic and Key Details
What key details tell how the egret searches for food in a pond?

Brian Kanof/McGraw-Hill Education

Informational Text: This genre tells about real people, places, things, or events by presenting facts about them. Informational texts sometimes use maps to give information.

Informational Text

What real thing are you learning about?

Main Topic and Key Details

Think Aloud

We've learned that knowing the main topic and key details can help us understand the text. This selection is about using maps to help us find different places. A key detail I read is that maps are everywhere—even on our phones. Let's listen for other key details as we read.

location: a place

represent: show something

Follow the Map

If your family is driving to a new town and gets lost, what can they use to help them? A map. If you need to find your way around a zoo, what can help you? A map. If you want to find the **location** of a country or city around the world, where can you look? A map!

Maps are everywhere—in books, on your computer, even on a phone. Let's take a closer look at this helpful tool.

Take a peek around your classroom. Now imagine drawing a big rectangle on a piece of paper to **represent** your classroom. Next draw a small picture of each main item you see—desks, tables, computers, and more. This drawing you made is a map.

A map shows the features of an area. Look at the map below. Do you see all the pictures in the boxes on it? Maps use special pictures called symbols to give you information. Symbols stand for real things found in the world. For example, a tree on a map could be a symbol for a big forest.

But how do you know what the symbols mean? Most maps have a special box called a key that explains what the symbols mean.

Look at the different places on the map and in the key. The symbols and key help you find things. What does the ice skates symbol mean? What about the symbol of a slide? Trace a path from the playground to the basketball court. Then find your way from the basketball court to the soccer field. Guess what—you just used a map!

How might a family coming to this park use this map?

Reread

Think Aloud

Remember that we can reread the text if we don't understand something. I don't understand what the ice skates symbol means. Then I reread the first paragraph. It says that symbols stand for real things found in the world. So the ice skates symbol stands for a skating rink. Let's continue reading. If you don't understand something, ask me to stop and I will reread it.

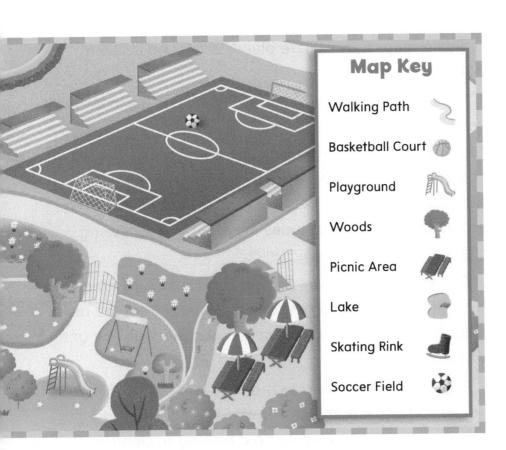

Map Key

Walking Path

Basketball Court

Playground

Woods

Picnic Area

Lake

Skating Rink

Soccer Field

Another type of map you may see is a building map. Building maps show where places are found inside a building.

Let's look at one. This map is of a school. It shows the school from above. It's like you are a bird flying over the school and looking down. You can see that the map shows the different classrooms, the gymnasium where kids play, the principal's office, and the music room. This school building map includes the hallway **connecting** the different rooms, too.

Can you find your way around this school? It's time for lunch. How would you get to the cafeteria from the main **entrance**? After lunch, you have music. How do you get to the music room?

Oh, no! You are called to the principal's office. How would you get there? Don't worry! She just wants to tell you what a good job you did helping to clean the playground.

connecting: linking one thing to another

entrance: the way into a place

Main Topic and Key Details
What key details do you learn about school maps?

Reread
Remember to ask me to reread any parts of the text that you don't understand.

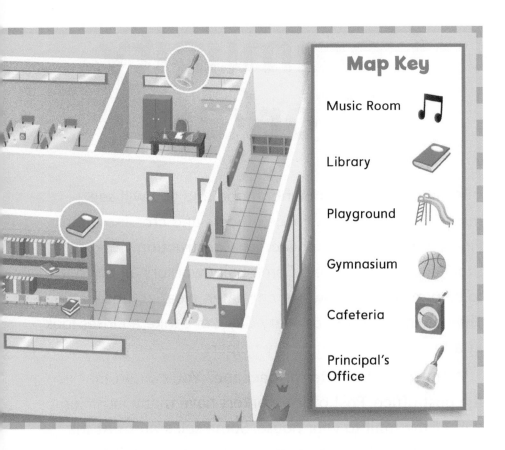

Map Key

Music Room

Library

Playground

Gymnasium

Cafeteria

Principal's Office

The bell rings, and school is over. You can't wait to get outside and enjoy the bright sunshine! How do you leave the school? You go out through the front entrance. It's a good thing you have a map to help you find your way! And when you're outside, you can use the map to find a place to play.

How can a map of a school be an important tool for children, teachers, and school staff? How might it be important for parents and visitors?

Maps help you find things. They tell you where things are. They can also show you the best or fastest **route** to travel. Now that you know how to read different kinds of maps, it's time to go out and explore!

Main Topic and Key Details

What does a map have that shows us how to leave the school? How is this detail related to the main topic of this text?

route: the way to get somewhere

Genre

Informational Text: This genre tells about real people, places, things, or events by presenting facts and information about them.

pitch in: do something to help a group

Main Topic and Key Details

Think Aloud

The main topic is what the selection is mostly about. The main topic of this selection is community workers. On this page, I read that some post office workers deliver the mail. This is a key detail about a community worker. Let's look for other key details as we read.

Community Workers

Walk around your neighborhood and you will see many people at work. Police officers and crossing guards. Firefighters and trash collectors. Construction workers, shopkeepers, and more. Community workers all **pitch in** to help make your town or city safer, cleaner, and better. They do important jobs every day. Let's take a closer look at a few of these community helpers.

Want to mail a letter or package? You can do that at the post office. Post office workers have many jobs. Some deliver the mail to your house. Some sell stamps at the post office and answer customers' questions. Others sort the mail. And if the mail is going far away, it is loaded onto planes. So, in a way, pilots also help to deliver our mail. Who knew sending a letter took so many workers!

If you want to read a new book, there are many places you can go. Of course, you can go to a bookstore and buy from a bookseller. But, it is a lot of fun to get a free book. Where can you do that? At your local library.

Here librarians organize and take care of shelf after shelf of exciting books—books about dragons and princesses, books about wild animals or traveling into space, books filled with funny poems, and so much more. Just sign up for a library card and select any book you want to **borrow**. The librarian is there to help you. For example, the librarian can find a book on a topic you like, such as sharks. The librarian makes sure the library has lots of interesting books for everyone to read.

You can also read magazines and borrow movies at the library. Many libraries even have story hour, when you can listen to books read aloud or watch puppet shows.

borrow: to take with the promise to return

Reread

Think Aloud

Remember that we can go back and reread anything we don't understand. I don't understand what a librarian does. So I reread the second paragraph and learned that a librarian can help us find a book and make sure the library has interesting books to read. Listen as I read. You can ask me to reread something that you don't understand.

Informational Text

How does the photo help you understand the information in the text?

Reread

Remember to ask me to reread any parts of the text that you don't understand.

variety: different kinds

Main Topic and Key Details

What are some key details you learn about community workers in a diner?

What if your stomach is growling while you are walking around your neighborhood, and you want to get something to eat? A fun place to go is a diner, which is a small restaurant. Most diners serve a large **variety** of foods—from hamburgers to macaroni and cheese to tasty soups.

Many people work in a diner. There is the host or hostess. This person seats customers when they enter the diner. Then there are the waiters and waitresses. They take your food order and make sure it gets to you as quickly as possible. There are also the cooks, who you usually don't see. They, of course, make the food.

In addition, you have the manager, who makes sure everything runs smoothly and everyone is doing his or her job correctly. There are also busboys, who clean up the tables and get them ready for the next hungry customers who walk in the door!

Another place that has many community workers is your local playground or park. You might not always see the people who keep these places clean and safe, but there are many who do.

There are groundskeepers who mow the grass, rake the leaves, trim the bushes, and make sure the plants and trees are healthy. Trash collectors keep the park clean and safe from flies and rats that can gather on and around the trash and spread **disease**. And most parks and playgrounds have police or safety **patrols** that make sure people are safe as they play, ride bikes, and even have a picnic.

So the next time you stroll around your neighborhood, see how many community workers you see. Stop and say a quick "thank you" for all of their hard work!

Main Topic and Key Details
What are key details about groundskeepers? How do these key details tell more about the main topic?

disease: sickness

patrols: people who walk around an area to make sure it is safe

dictionary: a book that gives the meanings of words

Make and Confirm Predictions

Think Aloud

We can predict what the text will be about by looking at features such as pictures. After I look at the first picture, I predict that the text will be about things that have changed over time, such as telephones. What is your prediction? Let's keep reading to find out if our predictions are correct.

Things Have Changed

Some of the things we do today were done long ago, but with a different tool or in a different way. Let's learn about how some things have changed.

When your grandparents or great grandparents were your age, they could *only* make or receive calls with a phone. Phones were much bigger and heavier, too. Most were attached to a wall and had a long cord. If people wanted to take a picture, they used a camera. If they wanted to look up the meaning of a word, they used a **dictionary**. Phones from long ago did not do these things.

Thankfully, today's phones are much smaller and lighter than the phones from long ago. And they can do so much! Many phones are used to take pictures. You can even use them to look up the meanings of words.

1

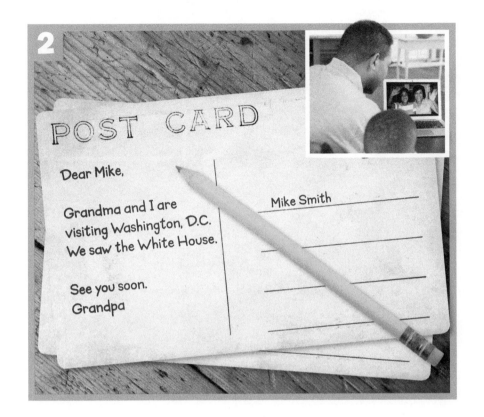

Long ago it would have taken your grandparents much longer to send a message to a friend or family member. Why? They would have written a postcard or letter by hand. Then they would have taken that postcard to the post office. And it might have taken days for the postcard to get where it was going. Maybe even weeks! Messages move much faster now. But hand-written postcards still **exist** and are a lot of fun to send!

Today, if you want to send a message to a friend, you can do it with the click of a button. This is different than picking up a pencil and writing! Now you can just sit at a computer and send an email. Within seconds your message will arrive at its **destination**. You can also type a message on a phone. This is called a text message. You can even make a video call! For this kind of call, you **chat** with someone on a phone or computer tablet and the person you're talking to can see you. Just remember to brush your hair first!

exist: are real

destination: place where something or someone is going

chat: talk in a friendly way

Text Structure: Compare and Contrast

Think Aloud

We can look at how authors compare and contrast different things in a text, or show how they are the same and different. I notice that the author compares and contrasts old and new ways to communicate. Writing postcards and writing an email are the same because they are both ways to communicate. They are different because postcards take a while to receive but you can receive an email very quickly. Let's keep reading to learn other things the author compares and contrasts.

(pencil) McGraw-Hill Education, (post cards) subjug/iStock/Getty Images, (bkgd) Marc Volk/Getty Images, (inset) Ariel Skelley/Blend Images

multiple: more than one

Informational Text
How do you know this is an informational text?

Make and Confirm Predictions

Think Aloud

Based on what I saw in the photographs on the first page of this text, I predicted that this selection would be about things changing over time. My prediction was correct because this page is about other things that have changed over time, such as bicycles. Was your prediction correct? Let's continue to make predictions as we read.

Bicycles are a great way to get around the neighborhood. Bikes from long ago didn't have **multiple** speeds, lights, or fancy tools. And people could only ride them on the road. Some even had strange handlebars and seats. However, like the bikes we have today, they were a lot of fun to ride and a faster way to get around than walking.

Today, you can buy a bicycle with 30 speeds! You can use your bike on flat, rough, and even muddy ground. And today's bikes might have things like lights and hand breaks. We also know more now about how to protect our bodies while we ride. Bikes have reflectors to help drivers see them. Bike riders also wear helmets. They may wear knee pads and elbow pads, too.

H. Armstrong Roberts/Alamy Stock Photo, (inset) Ilan Shacham/Moment Open/Getty Images

Yes, things have changed a lot since your grandparents or great grandparents were your age. Just ask them! But in many ways things have stayed the same. For example, you might play with different kinds of building blocks. Guess what? Long ago, kids also built things with blocks. You might create pictures with different kinds and colors of paint. Kids painted pictures long ago, too.

It will be interesting to see how things change in the future. Will there be easier, faster, or better ways to do things? What things will stay the same as they are right now? Just wait . . . you might be very surprised!

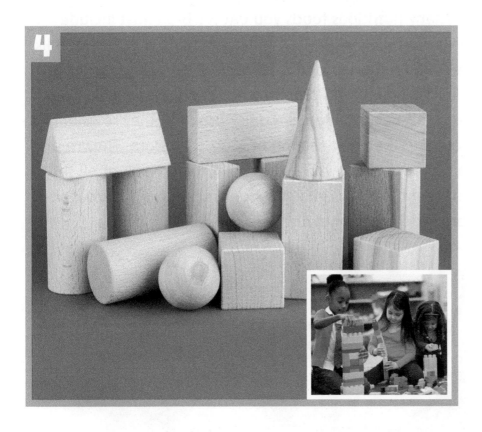

Text Structure: Compare and Contrast
What things is the author comparing and contrasting on this page? Find details to support your answer.

Make and Confirm Predictions
Have partners confirm the predictions they made.

Genre

Informational Text:
This genre tells about real people, places, things, or events by giving facts about them. It may use photos to give more information.

Informational Text

What makes this an informational text?

considered: thought to be

Main Topic and Details

Think Aloud

When we read an informational text, we think about the main topic, or what the selection is mostly about. On this page, I read about dairy products that people eat for breakfast. This must be the main topic. One detail is that cheese and yogurt are dairy products. Let's look for other details as we read.

It's Breakfast Time

Your body needs food to make it work and to help you grow. But did you know that breakfast can be an important meal? The food you eat for breakfast can jumpstart your body at the beginning of the day and give you the energy to think, work, and play.

Many nutritious foods you eat for breakfast include milk or things made from milk. Anything made from milk is called a dairy product. Cheese, yogurt, and butter are dairy products you probably eat every week. Although eggs aren't **considered** a dairy product, they're usually found in the dairy section of a grocery store. They're also a delicious and favorite breakfast food. Think of all the different ways to eat eggs—fried, scrambled, hard-boiled, or made into an omelet with cheese. Yum!

Image Source

So where do our dairy products and eggs come from? Often, they come from small or medium-sized dairy farms. These farms are all over the United States. Many of these farms are owned and run by a family like yours. A small farm might have 50 or more cows to **produce** milk and hundreds of hens to lay eggs.

Cows that produce milk need a lot of care from farmers. Cows are fed usually twice a day and are milked sometimes three times a day. The farmer must also work hard to keep the barn clean and take care of baby calves.

Reimar Goertner/Pixtal/age fotostock

Make and Confirm Predictions

Think Aloud

Remember that we can use features such as photographs to help us make predictions. After I look at this photograph, I predict that we will learn all about cows in the first paragraph. What's your prediction? Let's read the paragraph and see if our predictions are correct.

produce: to make

Make and Confirm Predictions

Think Aloud

I need to correct my prediction because I was wrong about the cows. The paragraph isn't about cows but about their milk, which we often drink at breakfast time. My new prediction is that the next section of this text will be about other things we have for breakfast. Was your prediction correct? If not, make new predictions!

3

Main Topic and Details

What is a detail about milk and eggs for families that live in or near a city?

containers: objects that hold things

Make and Confirm Predictions

My prediction was correct! We learned about how eggs, another breakfast food, get to the grocery store. I will read and look at the photos to see what happens next.

fresh: newly made or gathered

If your family lives in or near a city, there are many miles between a dairy farm and your breakfast table. So, it takes many steps to get your food. First, dairy farmers sell their milk and eggs to food companies. These companies take milk from the farms to factories, where it is put into **containers** or made into other dairy products such as cheese or yogurt. The eggs are also taken from the farm to factories and sorted, washed, and checked. Then they are put into egg cartons. Dates are printed on each carton or container to show how long the food will stay fresh. Finally, delivery trucks take the food to grocery stores where your family can buy it.

If your family lives and works on a dairy farm, the distance between the farm and your breakfast table couldn't be any shorter! The milk and eggs you eat are as **fresh** as can be. It's probably also true that your mom and dad make some of their own dairy products to feed your family or to sell at farmers' markets.

Anthony Lee/OJO Images/Getty Images

Many farmers travel to cities every weekend to work at farmers' markets. Farmers can earn extra money selling their products, and city people get to buy food directly from the farm. The food is at the **peak** of freshness. When people shop at farmers' markets, everyone wins!

Whether people live in the city or on a dairy farm, families prepare breakfast in similar ways. A big, country farm kitchen may look different from a small kitchen in a city apartment, but the breakfasts these families prepare end up looking and tasting very much the same. Delicious!

peak: the highest point of

Make and Confirm Predictions

Have partners confirm the predictions they made.

Tony Garcia/Image Source/Getty Images

Genre

Informational Text:
This genre tells about real people, places, things, or events by presenting facts and information about them. It uses text and photos to give more information.

Reread

Think Aloud

Remember that we can reread the text if we don't understand something. I don't understand why babies cry so much. I reread the second paragraph. It says that babies cry to let adults know how they are feeling and what they're thinking. Let's continue reading. If you don't understand something, ask me to stop and I will reread the text.

bitter: having a sharp taste

How Do We Change?

Six or seven years ago, you were a tiny baby who needed a grown-up's help to do almost everything. Someone fed you yummy food, got you dressed, and made sure you had a clean diaper. As time went on, you learned to walk, feed yourself, and much more. You changed a lot as you grew up. Let's take a closer look at some of these big changes.

Wah! Wah! You started out as a baby. When a baby is born, he or she can't speak. So how do adults know what babies are thinking and feeling? Babies tell adults they are hungry, thirsty, tired, unhappy, or need help by crying. Babies need a lot of help from adults. They can't roll over, sit up, or walk.

So what *can* babies do? They can tell the difference between sweet and **bitter** tastes. They can also learn.

1

2

Babies watch everything around them to learn about people, places, and things. For example, babies begin to **recognize** the sounds of voices and the faces of their family members. Babies can also feel love, and they love to be cuddled. It makes them feel happy and safe.

When you were about a year old, you were no longer a baby. You became a toddler. Do you hear the word *toddle* in "toddler"? *Toddle* means to take short, shaky steps, and that's exactly what toddlers do as they learn to walk. Like babies, toddlers are still growing, but they are stronger than babies and can do so much more. Most toddlers can hold a cup to drink milk or juice, feed themselves with a spoon, stack blocks, and make scribble drawings.

Now, instead of crying to communicate to their families, they can say simple words. Their favorite word is often "NO!" and they **repeat** that word often. They can also sing and imitate animal sounds. *Moooo!* But toddlers still need a lot of help from adults. Adults must watch them all the time because toddlers love to toddle away quickly to explore things by themselves. Be careful, toddlers!

recognize: to know when seeing or hearing

Text Structure: Compare and Contrast

Think Aloud

Remember that sometimes authors compare, or tell how things are the same, and contrast, or tell how things are different. Here the author compares and contrasts a baby and a toddler. I read that like babies, toddlers are still growing. A baby can't walk, but a toddler can. Toddlers are stronger than babies, and they can do more than babies. Let's keep reading and look for other things that the author compares and contrasts.

repeat: say again

3

Reread

Remember to ask me to reread any parts of the text that you don't understand.

Informational Text

What makes this selection an informational text?

imagination: the act of making something up in your mind

When you turned four years old, you changed from being a toddler to a preschooler. Preschoolers are much stronger than toddlers. Many can ride a tricycle, dress themselves, draw pictures of people and animals, and cut paper with scissors. They can also be very chatty. They love to ask questions to find out why and how things work in the world around them.

And a preschooler has a big **imagination**. When you were in preschool, you probably loved to pretend to be community workers like teachers, doctors, firefighters, and astronauts. One important thing preschoolers learn is how to follow rules. They also learn how to take turns and share. There's nothing better than sharing with a friend!

KidStock/Getty Images

Now you're at least six or seven years old. You're in school and sharing a lot. School-age kids are quite grown up compared with when they were babies, toddlers, and preschoolers. They can pay attention to their teacher and do class work for a longer time than they could when they were preschoolers. They can also recognize more words and read short books. Many enjoy learning new things like ballet or soccer. Maybe you do, too!

All kids change as they grow. You **certainly** did. Think about all the ways you've changed and all the new things you've learned to do since you were a baby. Now imagine all of the wonderful things you'll be able to do as you keep growing.

**Text Structure:
Compare and
Contrast**
*What is the author
contrasting on this
page? Find details to
support your answer.*

certainly: surely

Welcome to Prairie Dog Town!

Have you ever seen a prairie dog? You may have if you live in the part of our country known as the Great Plains. These grassy areas are also called prairies. Some prairies appear to be empty. But they are not. If you look closely, you will see **mounds** of dirt and little animals standing on them. These are prairie dogs!

Large groups of prairie dogs live together under ground. With all of those prairie dogs living in one place, they must do a lot together! Let's learn about all of the different ways that prairie dogs help each other and work together.

One way they help each other is by working together to build their home. Prairie dogs use their sharp claws to dig miles of underground tunnels in the dirt. These **fascinating** tunnels, or burrows, are sometimes connected to towns where hundreds or thousands of prairie dogs live. A prairie dog can travel miles underground just going from one town to another!

Each town has many chambers, or rooms. There are rooms for child care. Rooms for sleeping. Rooms for going to the bathroom. And rooms for storing food. There are even listening rooms near the entrance to the burrow, where prairie dogs listen for predators before going outside.

Predators are animals that hunt other animals. They can be a big problem for prairie dogs, and prairie dogs must listen for them carefully. Predators that hunt prairie dogs include coyotes, bobcats, and birds such as eagles and falcons.

fascinating: very interesting

Main Idea and Key Details

Think Aloud

The main idea is what the selection is mostly about. Key details give information about the main idea. I found a key detail: the prairie dogs work together to build their home. Let's look for more key details as we read. Then we will use them to figure out the main idea.

Ask and Answer Questions

Remember to look for the answers to your own questions.

grooms: cleans

Main Idea and Key Details

What is a key detail on this page? Use the key details to figure out the main idea.

Another way that prairie dogs help each other is by taking care of their young. After babies, called pups, are born, the mother and father take turns caring for them in the burrow. The mother provides food for her babies and also **grooms** their fur. The father protects the babies from other male prairie dogs.

When the pups are a little older, they can leave the safety of the burrow and explore the world outside. The mother prairie dog will watch her pups closely when they are outside to make sure that they are safe from predators.

One of the most important ways that prairie dogs help each other is by guarding against attacks from predators. Prairie dogs take turns with a **partner** standing on the mound outside the burrow and watching for danger. If the prairie dog on duty spots a predator, it barks a **warning**. Their barks all sound alike to us, but not to other prairie dogs. They make different sounds to describe different predators. For example, the bark that warns of a coyote sounds different from the one warning that a hawk is flying nearby.

When others hear the warning bark, they **scurry** back into their burrows. When the **danger** is past, prairie dogs on watch give a different bark that signals it's safe to come out again.

It's fun to learn about animals that not only live together but also help each other do many things. Prairies would not be the same without these smart and lively creatures!

Ask and Answer Questions

Think Aloud

I was able to answer my question when I read this page. Prairie dogs stand on the mound to watch for danger.

Informational Text
What is being described on this page? How does the author describe it?

partner: someone who works with another person

warning: a notice of trouble close by

scurry: run quickly

danger: something that causes harm

Informational Text: This genre tells about real people, places, things, or events by presenting facts and information about them. It may use illustrations or photos to provide information.

Main Idea and Key Details

Think Aloud

Remember that as we read, we look for details that tell about the main idea, or what the selection is mostly about. One key detail I read on this page is that some animals keep warm by growing extra feathers or fur. Let's continue looking for key details as we read.

harsh: unpleasant and difficult to experience

Winter Warriors

"Brrr!"—winter is here and it's cold outside. So how do you stay warm? When you go out, you wear extra layers, like a sweater and jacket. If it's *really* cold or snow is falling, you put on your hat, scarf, mittens, and boots. At home, you turn up the heat and put an extra blanket on your bed. So it's pretty easy for you to keep warm. But what about animals that live outside—how do they survive the **harsh** weather?

Some animals migrate, or move to warm places during the freezing winter months. Others stay where they are and grow extra feathers or fur! Let's find out how some of these animals handle the cold.

Snow leopards live high in the mountains where the air is **extremely** chilly and strong winds whip the snow around. But this cold weather doesn't seem to bother these animals too much. Why? The outer hair on a snow leopard's fur coat is more than three inches long, and it has a thick, woolly undercoat that provides another **layer** of warmth. Their smoky gray fur with dark spots also helps them blend in with the rocky, snow-covered mountains, so they can hide and hunt all winter without being seen.

What other features of the snow leopard's body protect it from the cold? It has large, wide paws. These paws have thick, furry pads that help the snow leopard walk on snow, like snowshoes. And last, but not least, a resting snow leopard can wrap its long, fluffy tail around its body like a warm scarf!

extremely: much more than usually

layer: something that covers an area and lies over or under another

Ask and Answer Questions

Think Aloud

Remember that we can ask ourselves questions about the text as we read. I wonder how the snow leopard stays warm. I will keep reading to see if my question is answered. As I read, think of questions you have and then listen for the answers.

Ask and Answer Questions

Think Aloud

I noticed the answer to my question. The animal's fur is long. Under the fur is something called an undercoat, so the animal has two layers to stay warm. Remember to look for the answers to your own questions.

Informational Text
What information can we learn from the photograph?

energy: the ability to be active

barrier: something that keeps things apart

seek: look for

Main Idea and Key Details
What key detail tells about how fish survive a harsh winter? Think about the information that is most important.

Closer to home, ponds and lakes have animals living in them, too. In winter, when temperatures drop below freezing, you've probably noticed that many lakes are covered with ice. Maybe you've also wondered what happens to the fish.

You'll be happy to know that fish can survive under an ice-covered pond or lake for several months. How do they do that? In fall, they eat lots of food and store enough **energy** to live until spring. The ice on top of the lake is like a **barrier** that keeps the water below from freezing. The fish then **seek** a good spot and stay there for the winter. Often, they settle in deeper water where the temperature is warmer. Their bodies slow down, and they hardly move throughout the winter season.

In spring, the ice melts and plants begin growing in shallow areas of the water. The fish seem to burst back to life and start moving. They swim to shallow waters to **search** for plants to eat. Imagine how good it must feel to move and eat again.

Now that you know how some animals survive winter, you can appreciate how easy you have it. The next time it's cold outside and you're cozy at home with a cup of hot cocoa, think about the snow leopard in the mountains and the fish in the lakes. Wish them well and hope for an early spring!

Main Idea and Key Details

What is one key detail in the first paragraph? Use the key details you've learned to figure out the main idea.

search: look for

Huntstock/Getty Images

Service Dogs

Dogs are called "man's best friend." But did you know that dogs are also great helpers? Some dogs work with people who have special needs, such as persons who are **blind** or visually impaired. Other dogs work with the police and firefighters to protect us. These service dogs have very **important** jobs. Let's find out more about how these dogs help!

Seeing-Eye Dogs

Dogs that work with blind and visually impaired persons are called seeing-eye dogs. These dogs are trained to help people get around safely. In the United States there are over 60,000 blind and visually impaired kids in schools. These kids need seeing-eye dogs to help them move from place to place. But how do these dogs know what to do?

Seeing-eyes dogs are selected for this important job when they are puppies. That's when their training begins. First these dogs go to special classes. There they learn **commands,** such as *sit, come, forward, hup-up* (which means "hurry"), and *steady* (which means "slow down"). Once they learn commands, they are ready to practice.

Their trainer puts a special leash and jacket on the puppies so everyone knows they are "on-the-job." Then the trainer takes them on the streets, and in and around buildings. The dogs learn how to be comfortable in these different places and around different people. They learn how to **guide** people around dangerous spots, such as street corners where cars are zooming by. They also learn how to guide a person up and down stairs. And most of all, they learn to stay calm in all situations. After months of training, these **clever** dogs graduate from school and are ready to work with someone who needs them. At last, they meet the person they will help. The two will quickly become best buddies!

Text Structure: Sequence

Think Aloud

Authors often provide information in sequence, or in the order that things happen. Understanding the sequence can help us understand what we read. I read that a seeing-eye dog is first selected, then trained, and at last, placed with a person. This is the sequence of events. Let's read the rest of the selection and think about the order sequence of other events.

commands: orders or directions

guide: to lead

clever: smart

Firefighter Dogs

Just like seeing-eye dogs, firefighter dogs have an important job. These dogs are trained to help firefighters figure out the cause of a fire. But how?

First, these dogs go to a special school for three months. There they are trained to **detect** sixty different things that can cause a fire. Once they learn how to find these fire starters, they are ready to work. Next, they are assigned to a fire station. When there's a fire, the firefighters race to put it out.

But that's not when their job ends. Firefighters must also determine how the fire started. When the fire is out and it is safe, they carefully enter the building. However, the firefighters are not alone. They may have the special firefighter dog with them!

detect: to discover or notice

Text Structure: Sequence

What does the firefighter dog do after it learns how to find fire starters? Retell the sequence.

The dog goes to work. It sniffs around the burned-out building. When the dog finds the cause of the fire, it sits down on the spot and looks at the firefighter. This is its **signal** that it has found the cause of the fire. The dog uses its nose to show exactly where the smell can be found. Finally, the dog is rewarded with a treat for a job well done.

People are very lucky to have smart dogs that have important jobs. Next time you spot a seeing-eye dog or a firefighter dog, think of all the special things the dog can do.

Visualize

Can you picture how a firefighter dog behaves when it finds the cause of the fire?

signal: a sign meant to give information

Informational Text

What real things are you learning about?

appreciate: think highly of something or someone

Ask and Answer Questions

Think Aloud

Asking questions about a text can help us better understand what we read. I wonder how a beaver makes a dam that is strong enough to hold back the water. I will continue reading to see if I can find the answer to my question. As I continue reading aloud, think of your own questions and then listen for the answers.

Beavers Are Builders!

Have you ever heard the saying "busy as a beaver"? It's true—beavers are very busy! Lots of animals build things, but beavers are some of the best builders around. So, what do they build and why? To **appreciate** what they do, let's think about where they live and what they need.

Beavers love the water. But they can't always find a perfect pond to live in. So they make one of their own! They do it by building a dam. A dam is like a wall that holds back water.

Picture a stream or river. The water is always moving. But when the water hits a wall, it can't keep going. So the water stops and forms a small pool. And that pool makes a pond.

Dams have to be very strong to hold back water so well. How do beavers do it? They use their teeth to chop down branches. Then they carry the branches across the stream and stack them up. The beavers add mud, which makes the branches stick together. They also add stones to make the dam stronger. Beavers use the **materials** around them to build the dam they need.

A beaver's body is very important for building a dam! While the beaver holds the branches in its mouth, it uses webbed feet to move across the water. The beaver uses its paddle-shaped tail to steer. Once the beaver is out of the water, the tail helps **balance** the beaver's body while it builds the dam.

Ask and Answer Questions

Think Aloud

I noticed some information to answer my question. The text says that beavers carry branches across the stream and stack them up, then add mud between the branches to make them stick together. They also add stones to make the wall stronger. Remember to look for the answers to your own questions.

materials: things found in and around a certain place

balance: make something steady

**Text Structure:
Cause and Effect**

Think Aloud

Remember that we can look for what happens and why it happens to find the cause and effect. I read that beavers make their lodge tall enough to rise above the water. This is the cause. Because the lodge is high above the water, it stays dry. This is the effect. Let's look for other causes and effects as we read.

rise: go up

section: part of an area

But dams aren't the only things beavers build. They also build homes called lodges. Why? Now that the beavers have a big pool of water all around them, they need a place to dry off! So they make a pile of branches, mud, and stones in the middle of the pond. They make the pile tall enough to **rise** high above the water, so the lodge stays dry.

This **section** of the beaver's world is important because not only does it give the beavers a dry place to rest, but it also gives them a place to store food.

When it's time for beavers to go to bed, the lodge makes a cozy, dry home to sleep in. A whole beaver family can cuddle up inside to stay warm!

Beavers also build a special feature for their lodges: secret **tunnels** that lead into the water from the inside of the lodge. Why do beavers need to be so sneaky? Animals like hawks and foxes hunt beavers to eat. So if a beaver sees a hungry animal, it can disappear under the water and swim right up to its safe home without being seen. The tunnels are also a perfect place for baby beavers to learn how to swim. The babies can be in the water while staying hidden from animals that might want to eat them.

Once beavers build their dams and lodges, they don't stay perfect forever. Just like people's houses, things break! So beavers are always working to fix their **structures** and keep them strong.

So now you understand how busy beavers really are. They are amazing builders that work hard to get the job done!

tunnels: paths under the ground or water

structures: buildings

Text Structure: Cause and Effect
We read how beavers protect themselves from other animals. What is the cause, and what is the effect?

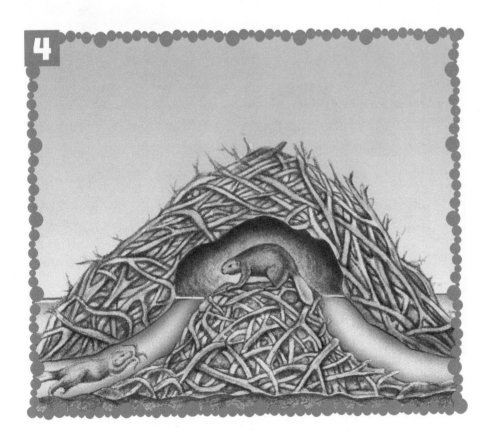

Genre

Author's Purpose

Think Aloud

When we read, we should think about details the author includes. This can help us identify the author's purpose, or the reason the author wrote the selection. I read that teachers can help us learn how to read and write. That detail can help us figure out the author's purpose. Let's look for other details.

accept: to take what is offered

noticed: given your attention to

Helpers All Around

We all need to **accept** help at times. Our moms, dads, and sometimes our grandparents help us get ready for school each morning. Our teachers help us learn how to read and write and do math. Our doctors help us to stay healthy. And our friends help us to have fun. Helpers are all around us. Some of these helpers in our community have an especially important job. They help us to stay safe. Have you **noticed** these helpers and what they do? Let's find out.

Some of us ride a bus to school. Bus drivers help us get to school safely. Bus drivers get special training to drive their big yellow bus, which is larger and longer than a car. They must drive carefully, and they must keep their eyes on all the kids on the bus. That's not easy! To keep us safe, bus drivers make rules such as "stay in your seat," "talk quietly," and "keep the **aisle** clear of backpacks and other things."

Like bus drivers, school crossing guards help kids get to school safely. Some of us walk to school. We must go across busy streets that **often** have lots of cars **zooming** by. The crossing guard holds up his or her hand to stop the traffic and guides us across the street *only* when it's safe. Crossing guards wear a special vest as part of their uniform. Everyone can see it, and it helps to keep them safe while they stand in the street.

aisle: a path between two things

often: many times

zooming: moving very fast

Reread

Think Aloud

The first time I read this page, I didn't understand why the author used the word only. *I reread and understood the crossing guard* only *guides students across the street when it's safe. Listen as I continue reading. If you don't understand something, ask me to stop and reread that part of the text.*

Reread

Remember to ask me to reread any parts of the text that you don't understand.

Author's Purpose

Think Aloud

I'm still looking for clues that help me learn the author's purpose. In this paragraph, I read that the principal helps keep us safe in school. This is another clue to help me understand why the author wrote the selection.

enforce: make people follow the rules

Informational Text

What is the author describing in this paragraph? How does the author describe it?

Once in school, other people are responsible for keeping us safe. The principal, for example, makes sure we know the school's safety rules. We learn what to do during a fire, tornado, earthquake, or some other emergency. We also learn how to walk safely in and around the school. The principal helps to **enforce** these rules to keep all of us safe throughout the day.

But what happens if we get hurt at school? A school nurse helps to keep us safe and healthy. He or she can bandage an injured arm or leg. A school nurse can make sure a student who needs medicine takes it on time. He or she also teaches us about healthy habits such as washing our hands, brushing our teeth, and how to not spread germs when we cough or sneeze.

Steve Hix/Fuse/Corbis/Getty Images

Outside of school, many other people work hard to keep us safe. We see these helpers in our neighborhoods. For example, lifeguards work at swimming pools and lakes. They make sure we are safe when we swim and splash around in the water. They keep their eyes on the water at all times, searching for people who need help. If the weather suddenly turns bad or someone gets hurt, sick, or almost drowns, the lifeguard knows exactly what to do . . . and fast! Lifeguards get special training in saving lives.

Police officers also get special training. They help us by making sure our neighborhoods are safe from danger. If anything dangerous happens, they are quick to step in and keep us safe. They also come to school and teach us about safety in our homes.

All these helpers around us work hard to keep us safe every day. What can we do? **Obey** the rules and give them all a big "thank you!"

obey: follow, carry out

Author's Purpose
Think about the clues we found. Why do you think the author wrote the selection?

Holidays to Remember

Let's celebrate! Those are words everyone loves to hear. Each year we celebrate many holidays in the United States. The origins of these special days differ. Some holidays were created to remember important people and dates in the history of our **nation**, while others are the result of wanting to celebrate the lives of **ordinary** Americans.

On some holidays we eat special foods, go to parades, and spend time with our families and friends. Most people don't have to go to work on these days. For many holidays, we do the same things each year such as send cards, give gifts, or plant trees. And, of course, there are holidays when we get the day off from school! Let's take a look at a few holidays we love to celebrate and explore why they are so special!

Holidays, such as Mother's Day, Father's Day, and Grandparents Day, celebrate the people in our lives. We have the state of West Virginia to thank for these holidays. All three began there. These special days give us a chance to show our moms, dads, and grandparents just how much they mean to us.

Mother's Day is celebrated in May. It began when Anna Jarvis wanted to **honor** moms and all they do for their families. On Mother's Day you might make your mom a yummy breakfast, give her a card or gift, and do **chores** around the house so she can rest and relax. In June, we celebrate Father's Day. A woman named Sonora Dodd thought of the holiday to honor her own father. On this day you might give your dad a special gift, make him a card, and do chores around the house so he can relax.

National Grandparents Day, introduced by Marian McQuade in 1970, is celebrated in September. A flower called the forget-me-not was chosen as the official flower of this special day. We should never forget our grandparents and all they have done for us.

honor: to show respect to

Author's Purpose

Think Aloud

Remember that we can look for details to help us figure out the author's purpose. I read about holidays that celebrate the people in our lives. This is a clue about the author's purpose. Let's find more clues to help us learn the author's purpose.

chores: small jobs done regularly in the home

Informational Text
What information can you learn from the photo?

bravery: the quality of showing courage

Reread
Remember to ask me to reread any parts of the text you don't understand.

Author's Purpose
What information do you learn about Veterans Day? Do you think the information about Veterans Day can help you figure out the author's purpose? Why or why not?

Other holidays, such as Veterans Day, celebrate people in our community who have worked hard to protect our country and its citizens. A veteran is someone who had been in the military, which includes the army, navy, air force, coast guard, or marine corps. A veteran may have fought in a war.

Veterans Day really began when a war ended. To honor those soldiers who fought in World War I, the President of the United States created Armistice Day. This day honored the events of November 11, 1918, the date when the fighting stopped near the end of the war. Years later, the name was changed to Veterans Day and became known for honoring veterans of all wars. Veterans Day is still celebrated on November 11 every year. All over the country, people have parades, fly American flags, and thank veterans for their service and **bravery**.

Then there are those holidays, such as Presidents Day and Martin Luther King Jr. Day, that celebrate people who lived long ago. These famous Americans did important things to help **unite** the country and make a difference in people's lives.

Presidents Day is celebrated in February. It started as a way to remember the birthday of our country's first president—George Washington—who was born in February. However, now we use the day to honor all of our presidents. Most kids don't go to school on this day, and most banks and post offices are closed.

Martin Luther King Jr. Day is celebrated in January. That's because Martin Luther King Jr. was born during this month. This day **reminds** us about what he did to make sure all people are treated the same and have the same rights.

As you can see, holidays are special days that give us a chance to remember and thank people. Which of these holidays do you like to celebrate? How do you celebrate?

unite: to join together

reminds: makes you think of

Author's Purpose
What is the author's purpose? What clues helped you decide?

Courtesy National Gallery of Art, Washington

Sequence

Think Aloud

Authors often give us information in a text in sequence, or time order. Understanding the sequence can help us understand what we read. I noticed that in this text, the first thing that happens is Eleanor Roosevelt was born. She was born in 1884. Let's continue reading to learn what happens next.

shy: not comfortable around people

famous: well known

Eleanor Takes Charge!

She was born in 1884. She was a **shy,** serious girl who almost never smiled. She didn't think she was as pretty as the other girls, either. But this girl would grow up to become one of the most **famous** women in the world. Who was she? Her name was Eleanor Roosevelt. And she changed the world.

Eleanor was born in New York City to a wealthy, or very rich, family. Most people would have thought her life was easy. But when Eleanor was young, both her mom and dad died. So Eleanor was sent far away to London, England to go to school. There she learned that girls can do anything. She learned to think and care about the world around her. She also began to speak up for herself—something not easy for Eleanor.

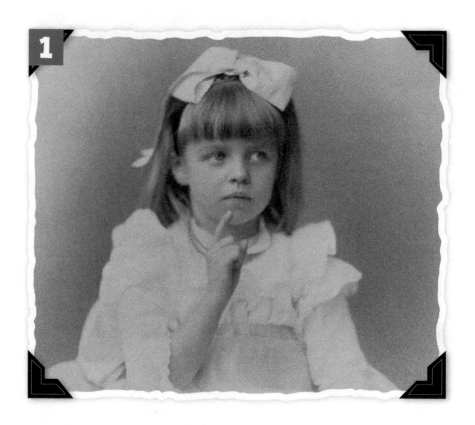
1

Corbis Historical/Getty Images

After Eleanor left school, she returned to New York City and began teaching children who were poor. She especially liked to teach dance. A few years later, she met a man named Franklin. Eleanor and Franklin got married.

Times were tough then. The United States was fighting in a big war. People everywhere needed help. So, Eleanor hopped into action. She visited hospitals. She worked in a Red Cross kitchen serving food. She even mopped floors and made sandwiches. No matter what Eleanor was asked to do, she did it. Helping others made her happy!

During this time, Eleanor and Franklin had six children, but Eleanor always made time to help others. But was Eleanor ready for what would happen next?

Reread

Think Aloud

Remember that we can go back and reread the text if we don't understand something. I realized that I don't know why Eleanor wanted to be a teacher. Then I reread page 150 and read that in school, she learned to think and care about the world around her. Listen as I continue reading. If you don't understand something, ask me to stop and reread some of the text.

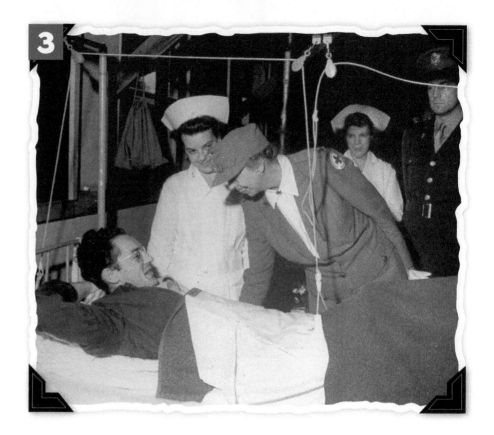

Biography

What is one important thing that Eleanor did when she became First Lady?

urged: encouraged

wounded: hurt

Sequence

What happened after Eleanor flew across the ocean?

Reread

Remember to ask me to reread any parts of the text you don't understand.

Eleanor's husband Franklin was elected the President of the United States. That meant Eleanor was the First Lady. First ladies before Eleanor had stayed quietly in the White House. People expected Eleanor to do the same, but she had different ideas. Eleanor would use her power as First Lady to help as many people as she could.

Eleanor visited coal miners, farmers, and factory workers, and talked to many families. When she returned from these trips, she told Franklin what help was needed and **urged** him to take action. In the White House, she became the voice for the people. And since the United States was at war again, Eleanor flew across the ocean to visit **wounded** soldiers in hospitals. She wrote down their names so she could write to their families. Letter after letter, Eleanor showed how much she cared.

Sadly, Franklin died near the end of the war. Eleanor felt her work was done. But then the new president gave her an important job. A new organization was started. It was called the United Nations. It brought people together from all over the world to make sure there would be no more **terrible** wars. Eleanor's job was to write a list of what this organization believed. This list stated that all people have the right to be free. It also stated that all people should be treated in the same way. Eleanor thought this was the most important work she had ever done.

Eleanor died in 1962 at the age of 78. When she died, the whole world felt sad. She had helped so many people in communities near and far. Eleanor is remembered today for how she fought for equal rights and the rights of women. And for that, she will always be remembered.

Sequence
What work did Eleanor do after Franklin died?

terrible: very bad

Garrett's Clever Idea

As you brushed your teeth this morning, did you wonder how something like a toothbrush was invented? Someone created the toothbrush many years ago from just an **idea**. Many people invent things that solve problems, such as the toothbrush. Maybe someone wants to make something work better or faster. Or maybe they have an idea for a product that has never been made before. An **invention** can do that.

One person who invented something that solved a problem was Garrett Morgan. He was a businessman who tried to help people with his inventions. Let's learn more about Garrett and how he became an important person in history.

1

2

Garrett Morgan was born in Kentucky in 1877. His parents had been enslaved. A few years after he was born, the first traffic light was invented. He spent his childhood working on his family's farm. He left home as a teenager to find work.

Over the years, Garrett had many jobs and started many different companies. He invented new products. One day, he helped to solve a traffic problem.

People started driving cars in the late 1800s. However, in the early 1920s, there was a lot of traffic. In cities like Cleveland, Ohio, where Garrett spent most of his life, there were also a lot of **pedestrians**. They didn't always know when to cross the street. Drivers and pedestrians didn't always see or pay attention to the traffic lights. What was needed was for someone to invent a traffic light that could control traffic and keep pedestrians safe.

pedestrians: people who are walking

Biography
How do you know that this is a biography?

Text Structure: Problem and Solution

(**Think Aloud**)

A problem is something that a person wants to overcome, solve, or figure out. The way the person solves the problem is the solution. We can look for problems and solutions to help us to better understand the text. The problem is that there is a lot of traffic on the roads and it's dangerous for drivers and pedestrians. Let's keep reading to find out the steps taken to solve the problem.

intersection: where streets cross

controlled: took charge

unusual: not common

After seeing a traffic accident at an **intersection**, Garrett had an idea. He created a traffic signal that would stop all traffic at an intersection. This way, pedestrians could safely cross the street. Then the signal would change, letting cars cross the intersection in one direction and then another. A traffic officer **controlled** the signal by turning a crank on the bottom of the light.

His **unusual** invention even had a setting for nighttime. At night, there wasn't as much traffic, and there wasn't a traffic officer working. So Garrett's traffic light showed a special nighttime signal. When drivers saw this signal, they knew they had to be careful and drive slowly across the intersection.

Garrett's invention received a patent in 1923. A patent is a document given by the United States government to a person for his or her invention. This document states that for a certain period of time, no one else can make or sell an object that is like that invention.

Garrett came up with ideas for other things, too. He invented a new kind of sewing machine, created hair care products, and even started his own newspaper.

Garrett Morgan died in 1963, but his traffic light invention lives on. Although the traffic light has changed since 1923, people still want drivers and pedestrians to be safe. We have **modern** lights that tell drivers to slow down, stop, and go as they get close to an intersection. Most city streets also have traffic signals that show when it's safe for pedestrians to cross the street. Why do you think Garrett would have been happy with these changes?

Think about how Garrett came up with his ideas. Would you like to invent things and help solve problems? Maybe you can be an inventor like Garrett Morgan!

modern: in the present time